THE EUROPEAN DIFFERENCE

Business Ethics in the Community of European Management Schools

THE EUROPEAN DIFFERENCE

Business Ethics in the Community of European Management Schools

edited by

LÁSZLÓ ZSOLNAI
Budapest University of Economic Sciences

Kluwer Academic Publishers
Boston/Dordrecht/London

Distributors for North, Central and South America:
Kluwer Academic Publishers
101 Philip Drive
Assinippi Park
Norwell, Massachusetts 02061 USA
Telephone (781) 871-6600
Fax (781) 871-6528
E-Mail <kluwer@wkap.com>

Distributors for all other countries:
Kluwer Academic Publishers Group
Distribution Centre
Post Office Box 322
3300 AH Dordrecht, THE NETHERLANDS
Telephone 31 78 6392 392
Fax 31 78 6546 474
E-Mail <orderdept@wkap.nl>
Electronic Services <http://www.wkap.nl>

Library of Congress Cataloging-in-Publication Data
The European difference : business ethics in the Community of European
Management Schools / edited by László Zsolnai.
    p.   cm.
Includes bibliographical references and index.
ISBN 0-7923-8262-5 (hc.)
   1. Business ethics--Study and teaching. 2. Business ethics-
-Europe. 3. Business education--Europe. 4. Community of European
Management Schools. I. Zsolnai, László.
HF5387.E939 1998
174'.4'07114--dc21   98-38358
                                CIP

Printed on acid-free paper.

Printed in the United States of America

TABLE OF CONTENTS

PREFACE

The book aims to present the *business ethics visions, programs* and *experiences* of member universities of the Community of European Management Schools (CEMS). Since the authors are leading professors of business ethics in different European countries, the book can serve as a special guide to the *European business ethics movement.*

The *Community of European Management Schools* was founded in 1988 as an association of top-level schools in management education throughout Europe. In 1998 member universities are as follows: *Budapest University of Economic Sciences, Copenhagen Business School, Erasmus Universiteit Rotterdam, ESADE Barcelona, HEC Paris, London School of Economics, Norwegian School of Economics and Business Administration, Stockholm School of Economics, Universitá Bocconi Milan, Universität St. Gallen, Universität zu Köln, Université catholique de Louvain,* and *Wirtschaftsuniversität Wien.* The *University of Economics* in *Prague* and the *University of Economics* in *Warsaw* are candidate members in CEMS.

Over thirty international companies joined CEMS as *corporate members.* Sponsoring corporations includes *ABB, Athur Andersen, Banca Commerciale Italiana, Banque Bruxelles Lambert, Banque Paribas, Cariplo, Central Hispano, Coats Crafts Europe, Coopers & Lybrand, Dresder Bank, Dunaferr, Elektrowatt, Ericson, Goldman Sachs, Grouppo ENI, Henkel Industries, Henkel Industries, Hilti Corporation, F. Hoffman-la-Roche, ISS, J.P. Morgan, KPMG DTG, Norsk Hydro, Petrofina, Procter & Gamble, Schindler Management, Schneider, Shell International, Siemens, SmithKline Beecham, Statoil, Swiss Bank Corporation, Tetra Laval, Trygg Hansa, Winterthur,* and *Zürich Insurance.*

The idea to produce a book about CEMS business ethics was born after the first meeting of the *CEMS Inter-faculty Group in Business Ethics* held in April 11-13, 1997 in Budapest. The *Business Ethics Center* of the *Budapest University of Economic Sciences* took the responsibility to organize this meeting where nine professors participated representing eight CEMS member universities.

Our book presents the business ethics activities of the following CEMS member universities: *Budapest University of Economic Sciences, Copenhagen Business School, Erasmus University Rotterdam, ESADE Barcelona, HEC Paris, Stockholm School of Economics, University of Economics Prague,* and *Universität St. Gallen.*

Some of the CEMS member universities are not represented in the book. *London School of Economics* and *Universität zu Kölz* do not have business ethics programs as such. *Université catholique Louvain* has a program in ethics and economics but its leader, *Philipe Van Parij* did not make a contribution to our volume. Also, *Franz Hrubi* did not provide a report about the business ethics activities at the *Wirtschaftsuniversität Wien*.

Regrettably, we were not successful in finding contact at *Bocconi Milan* and the *Norwegian School of Management* in Bergen as far as business ethics is concerned. Contrary to these difficulties, we believe, that our book can provide a *fair* and *rich picture* about the scope and degree of involvement of CEMS in the field of business ethics.

Papers of the book follow - by and large - the same structure. First, the authors present *state of the art* of business ethics in their countries and then concentrate on the *educational, research* and other *activities* of their *own universities* in business ethics, including the introduction of their centers, institutes or groups. Finally, some ideas about their *future plans* and *projects* are presented.

Not surprisingly, the character and the level of development of business ethics in the represented European countries and universities are rather *diverse*. However, *common characteristics* can be discovered in the business ethics experiences in *Denmark, Sweden, The Netherlands, France, Spain, Switzerland,* the *Czech Republic,* and *Hungary*.

Some *critical distance* from the *mainstream American approach* to business ethics is certainly a common characteristic of the CEMS universities represented in the book. European business ethicists are well aware of the progress and innovations that American colleagues have accomplished in business ethics but the relevance and applicability of the *American models* and *theories* seem to be *limited* in the *European context*.

European business ethics is deeply rooted in culture and less influenced by abstract principles or ideas - this is the main message of our book. In European countries probably *culture* is the main regulating force that provides a solid basis for ethics in general, and for business ethics in particular. Our book is an effort to demonstrate the *distinctiveness* and *cultural integrity* of European business ethics.

Budapest, 1998 April

László Zsolnai

ACKNOWLEDGMENT

The *CEMS Inter-faculty Group in Business Ethics* received support of various kinds. CEMS Executive Director, *Nicole de Fontaines* encouraged us from the very beginning. The *Faculty* of *Business Administration* of the *Budapest University of Economic Sciences* financed the first meeting of our business ethics group in 1997 in Budapest where the idea of the book was born.

We received continuos support from *Professors Károly Balaton, Sándor Kerekes* and *Miklós Virág*, the former and present CEMS representatives of the Budapest University of Economic Sciences. *Zsuzsa Krista* assisted us in many ways.

The financial contribution of the *CEMS Secretariat*, the *Budapest University of Economic Sciences, Copenhagen Business School, HEC Paris*, the *University of Economics Prague*, and the *Universität St. Gallen* made the publication of this book possible. We are grateful for this kind of active involvement of our institutions in business ethics.

Budapest, 1998 April   László Zsolnai

1 THEORY AND PRACTICE OF BUSINESS ETHICS IN DENMARK

Peter Pruzan
Copenhagen Business School

Is Something *Still* Rotten in the State of Denmark?

Although Shakespeare had good reasons in *Hamlet, Prince of Denmark,* for asserting "Something is rotten in the state of Denmark"[1], it is highly doubtful that the bard would have applied this epithet today with respect to status of business ethics in Denmark. Although there is much still to be done, Denmark is one of the few countries in the world where debates as to the social, environmental and ethical responsibilities of business have been so extensive and led to such heightened awareness and action, both at the societal level and at the organizational level. This development, mainly during the past decade, has taken place in a strong symbiotic relationship with the research, teaching and mediating activities in the field of business ethics at the *Copenhagen Business School.* The following five major themes have come into focus in Denmark since the beginning of the 1990's: the *"political consumer", ethical investing, corporate social responsibility, social and ethical accounting,* and *values-based management.*

---

[1] Shakespeare, W., *Hamlet, Prince of Denmark,* Act 1, Scene 4, circa 1599.

STATE OF THE ART OF BUSINESS ETHICS IN DENMARK

In order to provide a setting for the presentation of research and teaching in business ethics at the Copenhagen Business School (CBS), the article commences by considering each of these five themes and their practical impact on Danish business and the Danish society as a whole. Each of these themes has come of age due, to a great extent, to activities at CBS - and vice versa.

Enter the "political consumer"

The "political consumer" is a Danish phrase which was created in 1994. It is widely used and recognized in Denmark and is indicative of a new and paradoxical situation where political matters are dealt with in the marketplace. It focuses attention on a new form of consumer activism in an epoch where politics is being reduced to economics and where the market is a dominating arena for political decisions.

Time after time Danish surveys indicate that consumers are deeply concerned about the environmental, social and ethical responsibility of business.[2] What is interesting about the development of the term "political consumer" is that it has not been harnessed by particular activist groups but has been promoted by the media and is an expression of the heightened awareness of the role played by the individual consumer in his or her interplay with the business community. Since many individuals in today's highly commercialized world feel that power no longer is mainly in the hands of politicians, they react "politically" by reacting positively/negatively in their purchasing behavior to what they consider to be the ethical/unethical behavior of business. Not in a naive attempt to replace political institutions, but to supplement the workings of democracy and, indirectly, to send a signal to the politicians. It should be interjected here, that the word "business" will throughout not be used in a strictly commercial sense; when we speak of business and business ethics we will refer to both private and public enterprise, local governments, unions, hospitals, associations, ngo's etc.

According to a 1997 survey, 52% of the Danish adult population mean that consumer boycotts are a good idea when one is to express his or her attitude towards ethical questions. And 37% of Danish consumers have within the last 12 months actively chosen not to purchase particular products or products of a particular company on the basis of an ethical stance.[3]

However the political consumer not only makes his or her point via decisions as to what *not* to purchase, but also, less provocatively and noisily, by making *positive*

---

[2] Although the "political consumer" is not organised into activist/pressure groups, it should be noted that there is a tradition in Denmark for the disemination of critical information on such matters as product reliability and safety, the working environment etc. In particular, the *Danish Consumer Council* (Forbrugerrådet) has over the years been a most active watchdog and is actively engaged in dialogue with all major producer associations.

[3] According to the major Danish business newspaper *Børsen*, April 14, 1997, p. 8.

choices as to which products, productions forms and companies to support. This "positive" group is less vociferous, more stable and perhaps more influential. According to recent analyses more than half the Danish consumers belong to this category of political consumers. For the past several years, investigations indicate that environmental, ethical and social/human rights issues are of great importance to them and that such matters "always or often" affect their purchasing behavior.[4] The ecologically oriented consumers constitute the core of these positive choosers.

Both those political consumers who make their point by deciding not to purchase a product and those who do so by making a positive choice (and of course there is a considerable overlap between these two groups) are characterized by being better educated, wealthier and more critical than the average Dane - and are recognized as "trend-setters".

Perhaps the most publicized expression of the "political consumer's" power in Denmark was the decision made by the major brewer, Carlsberg, in 1996 not to carry out its investment plans in Burma after considerable criticism, in particular by the so-called Burma Committee. A decision which demonstrated the sensitivity of top management to the Danish public at large. It is interesting to note here a very similar result in Holland, where the brewer Heineken also made a decision to pull out of Burma - not just due to pressure from the outside. According to its CEO a major factor was also the attitudes and expectations of Heineken's own employees who put pressure on the company as they wanted to be proud of their place of work.

Words can be important for the way that we look at the world, and there is little doubt that the invention of the oxymoron "political consumer" has contributed to the Danish focus on ethical issues within the business community.

Ethical Investing

Another such new, powerful and unusual juxtaposition of words, "ethical investing", is perhaps the most recent perspective on business ethics to be the subject of major public attention in Denmark. This time however, the term is not a Danish "invention" but has been used internationally for some time. Its major appearance on the Danish scene was in 1996 although a rather subdued debate as to the ethical responsibilities of powerful investment groups, such as pension funds, had been going on for several years.

In the matter of a few months things exploded. First with respect to the situation in Burma where a major pension fund announced that it was selling its shares in the French oil company Total which was heavily engaged in Burma and refused to change its behavior. Then in spring 1997 it was disclosed that the well known Danish producer of pesticides, Cheminova, was involved in the production and sale of

---

[4] See e.g. Hjulmand, K., *Det umuliges kunst: Politik og den politiske forbruger* (The art of the impossible: Politics and the political consumer), Jyllands Postens Erhvervsbogklub, Copenhagen, 1997 chapter two.

4

extremely toxic products used by unprotected, untrained workers in Costa Rica.[5] After considerable debate Cheminova's management announced that it had stopped all further sale of the product until such time as it could be provided in a far safer form (in pills), presumably within a matter of months.

At roughly the same time Denmark's largest pension fund, PFA, publicly announced a set of ethical criteria to be used when making decisions as to purchasing new shares and to selling existing shares. According to its CEO, the rationale behind this move was complex. First of all was the recognition of the powerful role played by PFA in the Danish society. Within the context of Denmark's relatively Lilliputian stock market, it possesses a very large source of capital. Furthermore, it also represents a very large number of active and pensioned Danish citizens, in particular those who are better educated and more affluent (and who are thus more likely to be "political consumers").

But the rationale was not only based on domestic considerations. Management had decided to invest far more heavily than hitherto in corporations outside of the traditional areas of Europe (primarily Denmark and Scandinavia) and North America. While it felt comfortable - quite incorrectly as will be seen - in its ability to judge the ethical postures of American and European corporations, it felt that it was entering into a very different domain in such areas as the Far East. Therefore, it argued, it needed the ability to filter out the following two types of investment possibilities in these newer markets: those corporations which a) could be considered risky with respect to their future income generation due to an unfortunate environmental or ethical profile, and b) which were already characterized by the use of e.g. child/slave labor, by a gross misuse of the environment, by the production of landmines and the like. It was therefore decided to develop a data base and a screening system which could help the pension fund's dealers to avoid purchasing minor positions in the risky firms and to sell holdings in corporations presently characterized by poor ethical, social and environmental profiles. This, it was argued would not only operationalize fund's ethical policy, it would also, in the long run, contribute to maximizing the fund's returns. A win-win situation.

Although this move by PFA received a reasonable amount of publicity in the media, things really exploded when the pension fund was faced with the dilemma of how to tackle the following problem which occurred not in some far away company that PFA had only a minor holding in - but in a very Danish company where PFA held a significant position. The media had uncovered some extremely provocative information about the activities of one of Denmark's oldest and best known corporations, the East Asiatic Company.

In partnership with a daughter firm of a large English manufacturer of chemicals and pesticides the company was involved in the production of an extremely dangerous pesticide. It is illegal for use in Denmark and a number of reports have described it as having caused a large number of deaths and debilitating illnesses in the East Asiatic

---

[5] A rather piquant detail here is that *Cheminova* is owned by the research fund of Denmark's second largest university, the *University of Aarhus*.

markets where it is used by inadequately trained peasants. Furthermore, to make the situation even more volatile, the East Asiatic Company was to market the product in Burma, where all such agreements can only occur with the blessing of the brutal military regime known for its use of slave labor - and where confidence in such matters as the proper training of this labor in the correct use of pesticides was extremely limited. All of a sudden PFA found itself in a huge and highly publicized dilemma. It was a major shareholder in the East Asiatic Company. And this company was not a far off company in the east, but very much a Danish company - which appeared to behave in a manner contrary to the guidelines established by PFA regarding human rights and protection of the environment. To make a long story short, PFA, which until then had been proud to tell about its new policy, appeared to back down. It had been heavily criticized in newspaper editorials and by some well-known Danish business leaders for taking an ethical stance as a cheap marketing poise and not as part of a serious, well thought through strategy. At this point it announced that it would no longer discuss such matters openly and that it would not sell its stock in the East Asiatic Company since it had received a report from that company's management which satisfactorily answered the questions it asked.

The debates as to ethical investments continue and several major pension funds in Denmark are now in the process of discussing with their investors how, and to what extent, the hitherto only explicit measure of performance, returns to future pensioners, should be supplemented by ethical considerations. And if so, how? It is also interesting to note here that considerations are not just being given as to how to avoid having shares in companies which do not live up to some sort of ethical standard. Interest is also expressed as to how and to what extent policies should be formulated which give priority to investing in companies which promote products and processes which are attractive seen from an ethical perspective. To illustrate, consideration could be given not only to avoid investments in firms which are heavy polluters but also to invest in firms which contribute to improved environmental quality.

This parallels the development mentioned above as to the "political consumer". Not only are investors actively making decisions as to what not to buy based on ethical considerations. They are also moving towards making positive investment choices as to which products, production forms and companies to support. This development is in contrast to almost all of the debates in the media and most teaching in business ethics which tend to focus on *unethics*, that is, on business behavior which the public considers to be immoral and unacceptable, rather than on situations where ethics plays a positive and socially constructive role in business decisions.

Corporate Social Responsibility

The whole matter of ethical investing is of course closely tied to the nebulous notion of corporate social responsibility. It is not my intent here to reflect upon this notion academically but simply to inform about the important practical role it plays in very recent Danish business activities. In particular two events are noteworthy here.

The first is the active teamwork established in 1993 between a rather remarkable, heterogeneous group of five organizations. The group calls itself "Responsibility 2000" and consists of a major internationally oriented manufacturer of industrial equipment (Danfoss), the Danish National Police, one of Denmark's largest and most highly respected consulting engineering firms (Rambøll - started many years ago by a pacifist and a vegetarian!), the largest Danish bank (Den Danske Bank), and the Danish Boy Scouts Movement! The initiative was based on the Scouts' fundamental motivation: via freely offered and unpaid services to contribute to the development of youth into mature, independent individuals prepared to take a societal responsibility. Based upon this foundation Responsibility 2000 has developed a number of courses designed to stimulate reflection on managerial and corporate social responsibility. In addition, it provides consultative assistance to the Danish business community regarding such matters. The most recent expression of that teamwork is the publication of the book *Responsibility and Values*.[6]

A second major event which underlines the present high level of concern in Denmark for the concept of corporate social responsibility is a governmental initiative. The Minister of Social Affairs, Ms. Karen Jespersen, took the initiative to develop a series of networks between private and public enterprises and the ministry. The underlying purpose is to develop an operational frame of reference which will stimulate corporate management to integrate concepts of social responsibility into their success criteria. In particular to focus upon how to assimilate those groups of citizens who have been marginalized on the job market into productive employment in a way which serves the interests of all parties involved: the individual, the company and the society. Such marginalized groups include elder employees who may have difficulty in learning to use modern technology, the unemployed, the handicapped, political refugees, second generation immigrants and so on.

A basic assumption underlying the initiative is that it is no longer viable for either the corporate world or the government to rely on the classical distinctions between private and public domains. That if corporations do not assume greater responsibility for the needs of marginalized groups, they will, in the long run, undermine the healthy societal atmosphere which is a precondition for a well functioning market and well functioning companies.

This is to be seen in light of the temptation, stimulated by competition and the demands of shareholders, to consider employees as instruments to be used or discarded on the basis of their calculations as to their cost-effectiveness rather than as a most important stakeholder with its own rights, values and aspirations. And similarly there is a great challenge for government and public institutions. For many years government's role in the Danish welfare society grew and grew and grew. With pride and pleasure governmental institutions grew in tact with the increasing needs and demands of the marginalized groups of citizens who were not productive on the private job market. With the resultant extremely high levels of taxation, insensitive bureaucracies, and an increasingly alienated proportion of the population. The threat

---

[6] Poulsen, P.T. (ed.), *Ansvar og værdier* (Responsibility and values), Centrum, Copenhagen, 1997.

being recognized now by both the private and public sectors is of a development towards a society characterized by haves and have-nots, both with respect to work, wealth and self-respect. And by the resultant tensions, which can come to extort great influence on the whole atmosphere and quality of life in Denmark.

With this background, the Ministry of Social Affairs, in teamwork with a network of leading Danish companies, has initiated a series of activities designed to develop tools and processes for integrating marginalized citizens into productive work. In October 1997, the preliminary results were presented at the major international conference, "A New Partnership for Social Cohesion - International Conference on the Social Commitment of Enterprises", the first of its kind and a follow-up on the UN Social Summit meeting held in Copenhagen in 1995. The initiative will be followed up by the Ministry of Social Affairs in the years to come. The goal is to contribute to the evolvement of new forms of teamwork between the public and private domains. And to new ways of reflecting on corporate identity, performance and success based upon a more comprehensive notion of corporate responsibility than the current financial perspective permits and provides.[7]

Social and Ethical Accounting

The various distinctions employed so far are closely interrelated. It is for example difficult to speak of "new ways of reflecting on corporate identity, performance and corporate success" as we have just done without introducing the notions of accountability and accounting.

One of the approaches to the notion of business ethics in Denmark which has been implemented by a large number of organizations and is still a continued subject of debate, is what was originally, in 1989, christened "ethical accounting". Its creation is related to another Danish activity which has influenced the development of business ethics in Denmark, the establishment in the late 1980's of the Academy of Applied Philosophy. Discussions there as to the need for a broader perspective on organizational success than that provided by traditional financial accounting was a catalyst that stimulated researchers at the Copenhagen Business School to develop the concept of ethical accounting. And the enthusiasm demonstrated in 1989 by one of Denmark's major banks to contribute to its practical implementation provided the necessary "laboratory" for the development of ethical accounting.[8]

---

[7] This emerging concept of corporate social responsibility should be seen against the following concept which has dominated economic thinking over the last 40 years: "Few trends could so thoroughly undermine the foundations of our free society as the acceptance by corporate officials of a social responsibility other than to make as much money for their share holders as possible." (Milton Friendman, Nobel Prize Lauriate in *Capitalism & Freedom*, University of Chicago Press, 1962).

[8] In a Danish article from 1988 my colleague, the philosopher Dr. Ole Thyssen and I proposed the development of ethical accounting as a means of operationalizing ethics in an organization. The article, now available in English, ("Conflict and Consensus: Ethics as a Shared Value Horizon for Strategic Planning", *Human Systems Management* 9, 1990, pp. 135-151) was based on our work with ethics and with decision making contexts characterized by multiple stakeholders having multiple criteria for judging the performance of an enterprise. Our proposal was brought to the attention of the management of Denmark's seventh largest

8

Briefly stated, ethical accounting measures how well an organization lives up to those stakeholder values it has committed itself to follow. But it encompasses more than just a snapshot at a particular time; its design, development and interpretation contribute to an on-going dialogue culture where values become vital for the organization's self-reference. Compared to traditional accounting statements, ethical accounting comprises more values, addresses more stakeholders, and is developed, interpreted and employed by all the stakeholders. Therefore it is not objective. Rather, it draws a rich and informative picture of how stakeholders perceive their relationships to the organization and provides the basis for a learning process whereby values become integrated into the organization.

At present it is estimated that roughly one hundred Danish organizations more or less regularly employ ethical accounting as an important tool for contributing to organizational development and to managerial effectiveness. It is interesting to note that the majority of these users are public sector organizations; hospitals, schools, homes for the aged, local communities, city governments and the like. In fact, ethical accounting has been implemented within such rather unique areas as the care of the senile (in the municipalities of Aarhus and Copenhagen, Denmark) and in animal husbandry (in Denmark and Norway).[9]

However, while Danish industrial firms have been reluctant to implement ethical accounting, their interest has increased considerably in recent years. For example, the largest Danish employer's association "Dansk Industri" in teamwork with the major industrial employee's association "CO-Industri" have initiated a special benchmarking project in 1998 to determine to what extent an organization's implementation of ethical accounting can contribute to both organizational and personal development.[10]

---

bank, Sbn Bank or "Sparekassen Nordjylland" as it is known in Denmark. The bank is a regional bank primarily serving Northern Jutland with 71 branches in 19 regional areas and with roughly 1,300 employees, 200,000 customers and 60,000 shareholders, most of whom are customers. A year earlier the bank had begun to develop its "Code of Values" based on psychological theories regarding people's basic needs. The top management was keen on developing a perspective on management and organizational development based on the values of its major stakeholders and offered us the opportunity of using the bank as a laboratory for developing ethical accounting. The first ethical accounting statement was developed for the year 1989 and since then such supplements to the bank's financial statements have been developed each year. See e.g. Pruzan, P., "The Ethical Dimensions of Banking," in (Zadek, S, P. Pruzan and R. Evans, eds.), *Building Corporate AccountAbility: Emerging practices in social and ethical accounting, auditing and reporting*, Earthscan, London, 1997, 63-84 and Pruzan, P., "The Ethical Accounting Statement" *World Business Academy Perspectives*, vol. 9 no. 2, 1995, 35-46.
[9] In addition, a large number of publications exist in Danish on the theory and practice of ethical accounting; in particular reference is made to the following books: Bak, C., *Etisk Regnskab* (Ethical Accounting), Handelshøjskolens Forlag, 1996; Hjelmar, U. (ed.), *Etisk Regnskab: En ny form for brugerindflydelse og kvalitetsudvikling i den offentlige sektor?* (Ethical Accounting: A new way of developing consumer empowerment and quality in the public sector?), Frydenlund, 1997; Morsing, M., *Den etiske praksis: En introduktion til det etiske regnskab* (The ethical practice: An introduction to ethical accounting), Handelshøjskolens Forlag, Copenhagen, 1991.
[10] The cooperation between Dansk Industri and CO-Industri is called SUM (Strategisk Udvikling af Medarbejdere - Strategic Development of Employees) while the particular study dealing with ethical accounting is part of the project called KUMO (Kontinuerlig Udvikling af Medarbejdere og Organisation - Continual Development of Employees and Organiation). For futher information contact: SUM Sekretariatet, DK-1780 Copenhagen V, Denmark; telephone: (+45) 3377 9111, fax: (+45) 3377 9100, email: sum@login.dknet.dk

What is perhaps however the most interesting development is that which is taking place internationally - with a major influence from Denmark. This development began in 1994 at meeting of a small group of enthusiastic people from the UK, Italy, the US and Denmark who were enthusiastic as to the possibility of developing a common framework for various approaches to what is now called the field of social and ethical accounting, auditing and reporting (SEAAR). Unknown to the Danes who had developed ethical accounting, there already existed a recent history of attempts in other parts of the world, particularly in the US and UK, to develop metrics for measuring an organization's social performance; the approach was referred to as social auditing. And in the mid 1990's other people were developing methodologies similar to ethical accounting and with similar motivations.[11]

In recognition of the development that has taken place during the last few years, the Copenhagen Business School contributed to the establishment in London in 1996 of the Institute of Social and Ethical AccountAbility, referred to as AccountAbility. An underlying motivation was to develop a consensus on standards that can form the basis for securing a recognizable and assessible level of quality in social and ethical accounting, auditing and reporting. According to its mission statement, "AccountAbility is an international professional body committed to strengthening the social responsibility and ethical behavior of the business community and non-profit organizations. The institute will do this by promoting best practice social and ethical accounting, auditing and reporting and the development of standards and accreditation procedures for professionals in the field."[12] Recognition of both the growth of the field and its universality has resulted in a number of international meetings and conferences dealing with SEAAR.[13] At present, some of the world's major corporations including Shell and British Telecom have committed themselves to implementing SEAAR while others are in the preparatory phases.

There is considerable evidence that within the coming decade we will witness a continuous development in the direction of methodological and reporting standards, accreditation of accountants and auditors and perhaps even mandatory requirements for enterprises to supplement their financial (and perhaps environmental) accounts

---

[11] A key person in this development was Dr. Simon Zadek, Research Director of the New Economics Foundation in London. For a historical overview as well as a presentation of the motivations and theory underlying SEAAR, reference is made to the major reference in the field: Zadek, S., P. Pruzan and R. Evans, *Building Corporate AccountAbility: Emerging Practices in Social and Ethical Accounting, Auditing and Reporting*, Earthscan, London, 1997. In addition to the historical and theoretical sections it also provides nine case studies of applications in a wide variety of organizations in the US, Canada, UK, Italy, Norway and Denmark. It is primarily for people facing the practical task of handling, developing and implementing corporate social and ethical responsibility agendas although it is also targeted towards corporate stakeholders and an audience of students and researchers.

[12] For futher information on the institute contact The secretariat, *Institute of Social and Ethical AccountAbility*, Vine Court, 112-115 Whitechapel Road, London E1 1JE, England.

[13] A resume of the first *International Conference on Social and Ethical Accountability: Balancing Performance, Ethics and Accountability*, Nijenrode Castle, Holland is available in the special conference issue (nr. 5) of the quarterly journal of the Institute of Social and Ethical AccountAbility, *AccountAbility*, 5, autumn, 1997.

with social and ethical accounts.[14] If this is the case, much of the credit will be due to the many Danish enterprises which took the initiative to implement ethical accounting as an expanded, more comprehensive, perspective on organizational performance in the early 1990's.

Values-based Management

This umbrella-phrase covers much of what we have so far referred to as ethical investing, corporate social responsibility, social and ethical accounting etc. It is interesting to note at the outset that we speak here in the plural of values-based management and not in the singular of value-based management. The point is, that this perspective on management is based on a fundamental assumption that there is not just one value in focus - and not just one stakeholder (in contrast to the traditional approach to management which tacitly assumes only one stakeholder, the owners, and one value, efficiency/profitability).

Although little empirical evidence is available, I would venture that a large percentage of the leaders of Danish enterprises are consciously or unconsciously embracing a values-based perspective on management. This is supported by a 1997 survey amongst the 300 largest corporations in Denmark (excluding firms from the financial sector). Roughly 40% "of Denmark's leading companies feel that the debate on the ethical responsibility of private corporations will have a significant or decisive influence on their decisions, strategy and external communication within the coming two years" and that "within one year one fourth of the leading Danish enterprises will steer their operations based to some extent upon ethical values."[15]

Since the mid-90's a number of books have been written on values-based management[16] and the term, just like the four other concepts reported on above, has become part of the vernacular. Briefly, major motivations which have been provided for employing a values-based perspective on management are as follows:

(1) traditional power is becoming powerless in democratic societies with flat organizations,

(2) when organizations suffer from growth-fixation the distance between decision-makers and decision-receivers grows too and management looses contact with reality,

---

[14] Elkington, J., *Cannibals with Forks - The triple bottom line of 21st century business*, Capstone, Oxford, 1997 presents the persepective that corporate operations will not be sustainable even "if they meet economic efficiency and environmental quality standards, but fail to meet emerging social and ethical standards..." (p. 129). A major focus is on the role to be played by "sustainability accounting" which will integrate financial, environmental and social/ethical accounting.

[15] *Mandag Morgen Rating 97*, Ugebrevet Mandag Morgen, Copenhagen, 1997, p. 13. See too the section: "First analysis of 300 leading corporation's ethical engagement".

[16] See e.g. Thyssen, O., *Værdiledelse: Om organisationer og etik* (Values-based management: On organizations and ethics), Gyldendal, Copenhagen, 1997 and Petersen,V.C. and Lassen, M.S. *Værdibaseret Ledelse - et alternativ til styring, regulering og kontrol?* (Values-based Management - an alternative to steering, regulation and control?), Dansk Industri, 1997.

(3) the language of money is too narrow,

(4) corporate stakeholders have a right to be heard, and they demand that management listens to them,

(5) a values perspective is necessary to protect corporate reputation and to develop identity,

(6) clever, creative, responsible, dynamic and loyal employees demand meaningful work and harmony between their own personal values and those of the organization,

(7) it pays off.[17]

From a theoretical perspective, the concept of values-based management in Denmark has to a large extent been based upon notions of communicative ethics and self-organizing systems and there has been an implicit assumption of a relatively high degree of cultural homogeneity and of shared traditions and language. Denmark is characterized by just these and therefore should have excellent preconditions for implementing values-based management as a new and vital perspective on leadership and corporate purpose and identity. In spite of an increasing pluralism, partly due to the influx of refugees, Denmark is amazingly homogeneous compared to most of the wealthier countries in the world. Furthermore, distances are small, most organizations are small to medium sized and, again compared to most other countries, they are open and "democratic".

RESEARCH AND TEACHING IN BUSINESS ETHICS AT COPENHAGEN BUSINESS SCHOOL

This concluding section focuses upon the research and teaching activities at the Copenhagen Business School. Nevertheless, it gives a reasonable picture of the developments in Denmark as a whole, since CBS has by far the most active and extensive program in business ethics of any institution of higher learning in Denmark.

Research in Business Ethics

Historically, the major development of research in business ethics in Denmark can be traced back to 1986 when, rather miraculously, at my request my department received permission from the dean to hire three of Denmark's best known, respected and productive philosophers to contribute to the development of the school's research and teaching in systems theory with its emphasis on holism and self-organization. Quite an accomplishment at a business school. Within a relatively short period of time the newly established *managerial philosophy group* resulted in the development of a series of publications dealing with various aspects of the broad subject of business

---

[17] See e.g. Pruzan, Peter, "When value is more than money: on values-based management", forthcoming in *Business Ethics*, 1998.

ethics[18], in the development of the aforementioned "ethical accounting" and in an attractive environment for Ph.D. candidates and guest professors. The group, which has been expanded since its inception, is now widely recognized as the most vital philosophical environment in Denmark.

The second noteworthy development in Denmark was the award by the Danish Social Science Research Council of a major award to CBS to support research in ethics, values-based management and ethical accounting. The project had the horrific title: "Ethics as a wholeness-creating, self-organizing communications process and as a substitute for traditional regulating and steering in organizations". The project was divided in two parallel parts: "Organizational Ethics and Ethical Accounting" at the managerial philosophy group of the Department of Management, Politics and Philosophy, CBS and "Ethics as Substitute for Traditional Regulation and Steering in Organizations" at the Department of Organization and Management, Aarhus Business School. The whole project was under my leadership at CBS.

This project ran until summer 1997. It resulted in a significant number of publications, in the establishment of networks of international researchers. It also financed two Ph.D. projects[19] and two international symposia in Denmark. The research grant had a strong symbolic significance as well. It granted legitimacy to the research and teaching in ethical accounting and values-based management and to the managerial philosophy group at Copenhagen Business School. All of this resulted as well in important ties to the Danish business community and to a very large number of lectures, conferences etc. involving representatives from the world of business and CBS' managerial philosophy group.

A third noteworthy development in research and teaching in business ethics was the establishment in 1995 of the *Department of Management, Politics and Philosophy* (MPP). This development was indirectly related to the above mentioned research project which emphasized the role of philosophical reflection in the practice of management. Establishing a department with "philosophy" in its name was quite a revolutionary step for a large, well-established business school. In a matter of just two years MPP developed into the largest department at the Copenhagen Business School, and, according to almost all research measures, is the business school's most productive department. MPP is now actively engaged in a number of international projects and teamworks (including the aforementioned Institute of Social and Ethical AccountAbility in London), and has close ties with institutions doing research in values-based management in India as well.

---

[18] Typical for this development is the publication of the book: Jensen, H.S., P.Pruzan and O. Thyssen, *Den etiske udfording: om fælles værdier i et pluralistisk samfund* (The ethical challenge: on shared values in a pluralistic society), Handelshøjskolens Forlag, Copenhagen, 1990 and a series of articles on ethical accounting, the first of which dates back to 1988.

[19] The Ph.D. theses are: Bordum, A., *Diskursetikken og Det Etiske Regnskab - Principper for Ledelse mellem Magt og Konsensus* (Discours Ethics and Ethical Accounting - Principles for Management between Power and Consensus), Copenhagen Business School, 1997 and Jensen, F.D., *At Lede den Enkelte gennem det Fælles - bidrag til en praksisforankret styringsforståelse* (Leading the Individual through the Collective - contributions to a conception of steering rooted in practice), Aarhus Business School, 1997.

MPP has roughly 25 full time research positions, over 15 Ph.D. students (who are employed by the department and participate in its research and teaching). In addition, the department regularly hosts about five guest professors from other countries.

The department's mission is to be a Danish-based, internationally oriented department of management that performs leading edge research and teaching on the leadership of corporations and other forms of organized collective activity and their interplay with their societies as seen from economic, political, cultural and ethical perspectives. This is to be achieved not by imitating other departments working in the fields of management, strategy or politics, but by developing and communicating a distinct profile, which is based on the unique preconditions for research provided by the Danish society. The department will create knowledge which is relevant in a future knowledge-intensive society, which will not just aim at economic and technological competency, but will also embrace environmental quality, social justice and ethical responsibility. Therefore it will be necessary to include not only traditional economics perspectives on organizational identity and performance, but also the political and cultural/ideological relationships that characterize the corporate environment.

The following is an attempt to briefly summarize and categorize the *research* currently being carried out in Denmark regarding business ethics. First of all there is research being carried out at CBS as to what might be called "leadership virtues".

This research focuses upon those virtues that are demanded of the individual practitioner in a managerial setting and on the abilities of a leader to combine spontaneous, imaginative action within an event without dispensing with normative obligations. Secondly, there is the research at the Aarhus Business School on "tacit ethics". This research has as an underlying assumption that, dependent of course on the culture, values can be presumed to exist in each individual, that these tacit values in fact are immediately accessible as a guide to decision making behavior, and that attempts to make them explicit (e.g. as in the case of social and ethical accounting) will result in a loss of their strength as vital underlying causes of managerial behavior. Finally, there is the research being carried out at several departments at CBS on values-based leadership, social and ethical accounting, ethical learning processes/learning organizations and ethical investments. The starting point here is the opposite of that of the research on tacit ethics: Values cannot be presumed but must interactively be developed, a language of values must be developed and means of measuring, evaluating and communicating business performance from a values perspective will be vital to the viability of enterprise in the years to come.

The *teaching* of business ethics at CBS originated with a course called Power and Ethics, taught both in English and Danish. This course has now been offered for the last 6 years, both at the undergraduate level, and, with considerable modifications, at the masters and Ph.D. levels. It is based upon a series of classical texts and gives the students, who almost exclusively have studied subjects related to more traditional subjects in business economics, the opportunity to delve into some major philosophical texts from the early renaissance until our time. In each case, the texts are related to the world of business today.

However, the offerings of courses relevant for business ethics has grown immensely in the last two years. This is primarily due to one major and unique development: The establishment in 1996 of a whole new education program called *"Filosofi & Økonomi/Philosophy & Economics"*, better known in Danish by the abbreviation, FLØK. This program of study has its own budget, student enrollment, rules and regulations. At present the program consists of a three years bachelors program and a two year's masters program will be designed in spring 1998. Roughly 100 students start the program each year.

The new program is unique in its emphasis upon integrating modern economic theory with philosophical reflection and a sense of history. It appears to attract more mature students than the other programs of study at the Copenhagen Business School. Although the program is at the time of writing this article only 1½ years old, it is perhaps not too bold to describe its students as highly motivated - but at the same time in doubt as to their profile and as to how the more traditional students and practitioners of management and business economics regard them. The teachers do not have many doubts; their students will be highly sought after due to their communication skills, their ability to tackle problems dealing with social, ethical and environmental responsibility and due to their training in formulating and analyzing such problems based not upon a profitability concept alone, but on a wider repertoire of perspectives and techniques.

In conclusion, it can be stated that there is a strong interaction between the debates and actions characterizing the Danish focus on business ethics and the research and teaching at the Copenhagen Business School. It is not possible, or fruitful, to attempt to answer the question of which came first, i.e. whether the activities at the management philosophy group at CBS have led - or followed - the developments in the Danish business world. There is a symbiotic relationship between the two, much to the benefit of both. This relationship is so firmly established that there is little doubt that the current high level of interest in business ethics in both the corporate world and the academic world is not just a fad but will continue to grow in the future. There are at the time of writing this article (January, 1998) a significant number of new corporate projects underway, particularly dealing with aspects of social and ethical accounting, ethical investing and values-based management, and a number of new books dealing with business ethics will be published in 1998.[20]

---

[20] A typical example of such a project is the development of social and ethical accounting at the major innovative and highly successful international producer of pharmaceuticals, enzymes etc., Novo-Nordisk. A number of other firms have similar projects underway. Another such example in its embryonic phase is a project called "corporate stakeholder convergence - a benchmark research study of the world's best practice in corporate stakeholder management" to be carried out by the Danish-based international consulting company Oxford IPC in collaboration with the World Business Academy, USA and the International Institute of Labor Studies, Geneva. And yet another such example is the work being planned by the Danish Ministry of Social Affairs to follow up on its pathbreaking teamwork with a network of 16 well-respected Danish corporations to develop methods for contributing to the development of new perspectives on corporate social responsibility with respect to marginalized groups of employees. As to new publications,

project called "corporate stakeholder convergence - a benchmark research study of the world's best practice in corporate stakeholder management" to be carried out by the Danish-based international consulting company Oxford IPC in collaboration with the World Business Academy, USA and the International Institute of Labor Studies, Geneva. And yet another such example is the work being planned by the Danish Ministry of Social Affairs to follow up on its pathbreaking teamwork with a network of 16 well-respected Danish corporations to develop methods for contributing to the development of new perspectives on corporate social responsibility with respect to marginalized groups of employees. As to new publications, mention can be made of a book planned for publication summer 1998: *Etik i Erhvervslivet* which will provide a survey of the major themes characterizing the Danish debate on business ethics and will have contributions by leading academics and business leaders.

2 BUSINESS ETHICS AT THE STOCKHOLM SCHOOL OF ECONOMICS

Hans De Geer
Stockholm School of Economics

Business ethics was introduced as a specific topic at the *Stockholm School of Economics* at the beginning of the 1990s. In 1995, the *Center for Ethics and Economics* was established, which marked the start of a more substantial effort, not just in business ethics but also in public sector ethics and towards a more comprehensive perspective on business values and the relations between business and society.

THE SWEDISH EXPERIENCE

Business ethics is not new to modern industrialized society, but as a focus for an academic endeavor it is a novelty. In Sweden the situation in this respect is similar to the rest of Europe, but there are also some traits that are, maybe, characteristic for the Scandinavian tradition. In what has been known also internationally as *"the Swedish model"* a certain number of presuppositions are taken for granted, concerning business' social responsibility and the balance between the individual and the collective.

The Scandinavian model implies a structure, characterized by a fairly good relation between (the mostly social democrat) government and (big) business, a strong position for the centralized trade union movement and other similar corporations

18

representing other interests, and a process that is pragmatic, negotiating, compromising and goal-oriented. Given this structure and this process basic values have normally been taken for granted, e. g. the value of a peaceful societal development and the (principally) equal rights of every human being.

Certain values, however, have normally been quoted by all the parties involved in this societal discourse, such as freedom (though the definition of freedom to what, or from what differs between the parties), justice (though here also the definition varies) and security (though the parties normally have different opinion of the best way to achieve that social security). During recent times the value of flexibility has been remarkably upgraded by all parties. So it would not be correct to say that values are not quoted and valid in the societal debate in Sweden, but for a long time they (e.g. values in their normative quality) were defined as entities out of the reach of scientific study and therefore excluded from the academic discourse in the pattern-setting economic and administrative sciences.

The establishment of business ethics as a discipline, or at least as a topic for research and education at the academic level, can be seen as *breaking* with *the tradition* that takes time and efforts. Before turning to the situation within the Stockholm School of Economics, let us look at what has been achieved at *other universities* in Sweden. The "normal" interest in ethics at theological faculties and within the philosophical departments at different universities is not reported here. Rather, we deal with efforts within *applied ethics* that more directly addresses the economic life.

At *Uppsala University* there is a major research program, *Ethical Reflection in Economic Theory and Practice*, at the Faculty of Theology. The program is managed by *Carl Henrik Grenholm*, a professor of ethics, and covers a wide range of perspectives, including gender issues. At the same University, the Department of Pedagogy, *Iordannis Kavathatzopoulos* has developed a model for moral education on the basis of a *Kohlbergian* interpretation.

At the *University of Umea* there has been no institutionalized effort, but in 1996, *Ulrika Nyhlän* defended her dissertation in business administration, the first focusing on business ethics in Sweden.[1] At the *University of Linköping*, a Center for Applied Ethics had been established, managed by professor *Göran Collste*, and it has manifested a certain interest in ethical codes, both professional and organizational.

At the *University of Gothenburg*, a course in business ethics has been held last year by the Department of Economic History, but it is unclear whether this course in the future will be part of the standard offer of voluntary courses. At the *University of Lund*, professor *Lennart Lundkvist* at the Department of Political Science, has devoted a considerable effort to the ethics in the public sector that is closely related to business ethics.

---

[1] *Gott och ont inom afförslivet. Utveckling av ett etiskt perspktiv pa företags relationer med aktörer* [Good and Bad in Business. An ethical perspective on stakeholders relations], Studier i företagsekonomi, Umea Universitet 1996.

STOCKHOLM SCHOOL OF ECONOMICS: THE CENTER FOR ETHICS AND ECONOMICS

As it has been shown, there are various efforts at Swedish universities, but the Center for Ethics and Economics (CEE) at the Stockholm School of Economics represents the program that is most directly addressing *business ethics* with a certain permanence. The CEE was established in 1995, thereby institutionalizing and strengthening business ethics program. Its main objectives are to discuss and assess the traditions and value-bases of the western industrial society, as expressed in economic life. In doing this, the focus is mainly *descriptive* and *analytic*, rather than normative.

From the introductory presentation of the CEE, I can quote the following:

Modern business life calls for rapid and quantifiable results. Fresh ideas and creativity are called for. The intensity of modern work life increases and at the same time, its links to local society are getting weaker. Action is focused at the expense of reflection, and short-sighted goals tend to block the meaning in the longer perspective. Thus, economic activity tends to free itself from the embeddedness in a specific frame of time and space, context and responsibility.

An increasing individualism, a diminishing trust in authority, the fragmentation of traditional beliefs and dramatically intensified intercultural contacts tend to reduce the opportunities to find support in traditional and stable systems of values and norms. The individual reflection and the communicative process, the good dialogue, must be mobilized.

Business, and economic activity also in other sectors of society, with its claims for stable rules of the game, must be based on public trust. The moral that creates and keeps a society together, is not inherent in the nature of that society; instead it must patiently be brought to the fore again and again, especially in times of dramatic change.

The CEE works through three different channels: education, research and external information, including the establishment of a business ethics library. The ambition is to become an important source of inspiration, information and communication for those interested in the field of business ethics and business values. The CEE hopes to respond to a growing demand in society and business for information and instruction concerning ethics and moral in economic life. The CEE normally does not deliver the answers, but helps in putting the right questions and informs about the variety of alternative positions to moral issues.

The CEE aims at the building up of a long-range competence in the field of business and organizational ethics, through personal and organizational development, and by creating the resources in terms of sources of information and networks that can be put to the disposal of the business community and the public administration. Also, the CEE will guarantee the prerequisites for a permanent and critical teaching in business and public sector ethics at the Stockholm School of Economics and will also be a resource for other universities and schools. The CEE also provides the opportunities of doing research in the field.

Teaching

The Master of Science Program at the Stockholm School of Economics consist of a basic, mandatory part, which roughly covers the first two years, and a second part that gradually offers an option of different courses. In this optional section there is also the place for the topical course that each student has to take, i.e. specialization and a deeper insight in a chosen part of economics and business administration: it could be macro-theory, finance, marketing, accounting, organization etc. The topical course normally extends over a whole term.

In the introductory course also business ethics is touched upon, but not much time is allocated to it. Among the voluntary courses, a basic course in business ethics is offered. It is a five-week course, with lectures (normally about ten two-hour lectures) and some seminars in smaller groups. The lectures ranges from moral theory, the relations between business and society in an historical perspective, the external responsibilities of business (stakeholder theory) and the internal moral questions of the modern organization. The focus of the course, however, is on a paper that the students will write, normally in groups of three. The topic of paper is up to their own choice: the most important criteria is that they write about a situation, a problem or a dilemma related to business life that they find interesting and important for themselves and that forces them to stand up for their own values. The empirical basis, as well as the theoretical inspiration, is discovered by the students; the role of the teacher and the tutor will be that of an advisor and a resource person. This is a way of working with a paper that is different from what the students are used to write in other courses, since it regards their own personal values as an important part of the intellectual process.

Courses in business ethics are also planned that will relate to different topical courses offered. Courses are planned such as *Ethical perspectives on the financial markets* and *Ethics and marketing*.

There have been courses offered in business ethics at the level of *doctoral studies*, but they will not be offered on an annual basis. There are plans to arrange courses at this level as a joint Scandinavian effort, but these plans has not been realized yet. Tuition is given to a number of postgraduate students at the CEE; their fields of interest is indicated below under the section on research at the Center.

CEE has been engaged in different *executive development* schemes and courses that the Stockholm School of Economics produces for clients both in private business and in the public sector. Often this is in the form of shorter introductions to business and organizational ethics.

Our Center also offers a course called "Business Values" that is a part of the *mandatory curriculum* at the Stockholm School of Economics in *Riga*, Latvia. At the School a two-and-half year undergraduate program in economics and business administration is offered to students from the three Baltic countries. The School started in 1994 and the Swedish commitment will last until 2004; at that time, according to the plans, the School will be run by Baltic authorities and Baltic staff. The main objective for the course Business Values, is to introduce Baltic students to the value base of Western market economy and private business.

Research

During 1997/98 the following research projects are carried on at the CEE.

Hans De Geer, Ph.D.: *The moral processes in big Swedish multinational companies.*

How do big multinational Swedish companies handle the moral processes in the organization? In what way does the traditional Swedish, or Scandinavian, model influence the managing of values and value systems? Focus is on the discursive processes within the organization, including ethical codes and other instruments of coordinating values.

Another project of Hans De Geer is under preparation: *Ethics in the Public Service.*

The project aims at mapping the various efforts to (re-)establish a certain public sector ethos in different parts of the public administration - both central and local - and to investigate the needs and possibilities for offering centrally

Tomas Brytting, Econ Dr.: *Moral Competence At Work*

It is argued in this project, that the type of organization theory which builds on relativistic ontology has difficulties in making sense of the way moral issues appear in modern work life. The objective is to further specify these limits of organization theory, and develop an alternative, non-relativistic concept: Moral Competence. Theoretical work within the project will be supported by case studies and training experiences.

Class Trollestad, DD: *Human Oriented Organizing*

In the growing "knowledge society" work is being quantitatively and qualitatively or existentially intensified. Attention is being paid to the organizing and managing of deeper or more fundamental human dimensions: the personalities and basic values of the employees. An interest in existential issues has entered the discussion about work in the future. This research program combines an organizational theory perspective with view of life science perspective. It has three objectives: (1) To investigate the possibility to increase moral competence at work, and reduce the risk for morally induced stress, through organization design. (2) To investigate, through action research methods, how common values develop in an organization and to what extent this can be directed by managers. (3) To set up a discussion seminar with managers active in change processes aiming at more human oriented work organizations.

Postgraduate research at CEE includes the following.

Marie-Louise Bernström: *The Perception of Morality in the Advertising Agencies - Cultural Perspective.*

The objective of the project is to try to understand the ways in which the organizational culture of advertising agencies affect the advertisers representations of moral and ethics. The main aim is to try to understand how the morality of advertisers is created within the culture of the advertising agency and passed on to the staff of the organization. Furthermore, try to comprehend how the advertisers as producers of advertisements perceive their moral responsibility and competence. Finally, try to grasp the relationship between advertisers' values, ideals and norms and the culture of the advertising agency.

Ylva Eklund: *Moral, Responsibility and Competence in the Advertising Business*

The purpose of this study is to connect several theoretical fields in order to describe the staffs' opinion of moral, responsibility and competence within their field of work in the advertising company. Furthermore, try to understand how the moral is developed and created in social interaction with the surroundings in the advertising company. The objective, more precisely expressed, is to understand how the phenomena "amoral advertising" can be explained in a view of social construction.

Peter Norberg: *The Calvinist Church-Room and the Amorality of Financial Markets*

How does the ethic in society affect its economic life? How does secularization affect the public acceptance of and development of financial markets. Financial derivatives are abstracted from the production of physical goods. Is this a sign of decadence in capitalist economies, in a late stage of capitalism? The economic ethic of today will be compared to the religious fundaments of early capitalism, where the Weber thesis of ascetic Protestantism being a basis for capitalism is of main importance. Is the evolution of capitalism still guided by a Puritan ethic?

Jan Tullberg: *Reciprocity vs. Altruism as Fundamental Ethics*

The central issue is whether it is justified to see altruism as the highest ethical value. The long tradition of collaboration between altruism and manipulation has not previously been developed into a casual theory. Strong emotional reactions such as debt of gratitude and revenge, indicate possibilities for reciprocity as an ethical base for prosocial behavior. This project will test the correlation between reciprocal ethics and practical co-operation.

Information

The CEE takes an extensive responsibility to provide information about business and public sector ethics. The staff is often and regularly invited to give lectures or to participate in external seminars arranged by companies, public authorities and other organizations.

Attempts have also been made to build a Nordic network, *ETOS, Ethics in Organizations and Society,* devoted to the maintenance of professional competence within the field in the Nordic countries. The center also has links to *EBEN, The European Business Ethics Network,* and to *EPS, Ethics in the Public Service,* an international network.

Staff members of CEE are Professor *Hans De Geer,* PhD; Ass. Professor *Tomas Brytting,* doctor of economics; *Marie-Louise Bernström,* doctoral candidate; *Ylva Eklund,* doctoral candidate; *Peter Norberg,* MA, M.Sc; *Claes Trollestad,* DD; *Jan Tullberg,* B.Sc., and *Helena Kvist-Aslund,* administrative secretary.

3 "POLDER-ETHICS": BUSINESS ETHICS IN THE NETHERLANDS

Nel Hofstra & Luit Kloosterman
Erasmus University Rotterdam

Ethical problems in business are as old as business itself. But who can tell us what is morally right.

We can think of the *nature-nurture* question of individuals and the embeddedness of our first moral experiences within organizations (you shouldn't lie, steal, you ought to obey), we can think of the relationship between human beings and the environment and its consequences for the corporate management of environmental issues, we can think of the 'Homo Oeconomicus' and the lack of the moral dimension in profit maximizing behavior, we can think of law and regulations and the role of governments in the free market.

Happily there is no crystal-clear answer, no univocal solution to the question what is or ought to be morally right, no universal norm or value. A systematic analysis of morality should show that in business, ethics is implied by several assumptions and perspectives. A certain approach would prevent that ethics in business is regarded only as means to a certain end and not as a value in itself.

STATE OF AFFAIRS IN THE NETHERLANDS

Fortunately at the end of the 80s a shift in attention to business ethics was signalized within the Dutch education system. Since that time it is not unusual that Dutch students discuss all kind of ethical aspects within business situations. Also fortunately, Dutch academics set the first steps into a more systematic approach to deal with the subject of business ethics (A.F. *Brand, E.J.J.M. Kimman, H.J.L. van Luijk, H.J. van Zuthem* and others).

Issues in business ethics are nowadays discussed at different levels of the company: the employer-employee level, the management level, the strategic level and also at the societal level. The level and kind of education varies: management studies, business economics, environmental studies in universities, business schools and post-doctorate institutes. Not only theoretical aspects, but also its relevance to business practice is seen as important and vice versa.

More and more the subject became also focused on the fundaments of business ethics.[1] This development meant a rapidly growing need in companies in ethical decision making accompanied by a large body of literature in the field. Nowadays the domain of business ethics is developing into a mature academic discipline in the Netherlands.

The business ethics trend in the *Netherlands* blown over from the *United States of America*. The most convincing argument to accept the concept in practice was the idea that ethics in business decision makes economic sense. Even a mix of P's (for example Proud, Prudence etc.) has been developed in the US to convince managers of the easiness to implement it. Dutch business culture seems to be more skeptical and less practical. Dutch entrepreneurs prefer practicing 'arm chair philosophy' about norms and values within companies. To a large extent it still lacks a systematic embeddedness.

However the importance and implementation of the subject depends extremely on what business ethics claims or doesn't claim. As *Amartya Sen*[2] noticed: the importance is not only *Adam Smith*'s idea that 'regards to our own interests' is an efficient motivation for exchange, but there are also economic relationships other than exchange.[3] For example production institutions and distribution arrangements. This means that not just the individual motivation, but also the organization and its behavior are subject to business ethics. In fact, the idea of corporate responsibility again comes into vision. And with it's counterpart the concept of corporate accountability.

---

[1] A.F. Brand, Kimman E, Luyk van H.J.L., Wempe J. *Bedrijfsethiek in Nederland*; het Spectrum Utrecht 1989.

[2] Amartya Sen: "Does Business Ethics Make Economic Sense?" *Business Ethics Quarterly*, January 1993, Vol. 3, Issue 1.

[3] Hardly any attempt has been made till now to develop a theory of moral sensibility on the base of Adam Smith's 'The Theory of Moral Sentiments'. In the Netherlands E.Brugmans (Morele Sensibiliteit; over de moraalfilosofie van Adam Smith, Tilburg University Press 1989) developed a theory on the basis of Smith's analysis.

It is recognizable that the concept of *'corporate responsibility'* which is traditionally more accepted in the Netherlands since the 70s will revive again. This time it gets a face-lift within the concept of *'corporate governance'*. But in fact founders of Dutch industry already showed their social conscience in the nineteenth century (*van Marken Gist Brocades, Anton Philips, Petrus Regout, Anton Plesman, Charles Stork, Tony Fokker* et al).[4]

It is necessary that some central questions will be posed. What is business ethics, how can we define the concept? How does a business ethical decision process go off, who discuss it and why and where? Norms and values often function as support to other mechanisms like authority, power or legitimacy. Debunking the sacred sacraments can expose the false or exaggerated claims and pretensions. The Dutch society can be characterized as pluralistic and multicultural and is implementing (too?) rapidly new norms and values into old ones. This implies a continuous change and shift in norms and in values, with the risk of societal instabilities and anomie. We can recognize the risks and dangers when business ethics contributes to the realization of societal values and ideals. A change in ethics from utility to virtue can lead to fundamental societal changes and will affect the moral legitimacy of market mechanism: the ultimate order to divide individual and collective behavior. In Holland the government is withdrawing more and more to broaden business space on the one hand, whereas on the other hand more responsibilities (and accountabilities) of companies are required.

The proud of Dutch politicians on our economic polder-model[5] is also manifest in a business ethics sense. That's why we call the Dutch type of business ethics: a *polder-model approach*.

DUTCH BUSINESS ETHICS: A POLDER-MODEL APPROACH

The polder-model approach in business ethics refers to a deliberate way of decision making. This means a carefully thought out way to consider ethical dilemmas in business. As a consequence the decision itself is lacking rapidity although purposed in the long run. The process itself is slow because of the need to estimate the weight or force of arguments or the probable consequences of a measure in order to make a choice or prepare an already taken (often implicit or hidden) decision.

This type of business ethics can be characterized as intentional. Advantages are the considerations and deliberations preceding a certain decision in order to consider and examine the reasons for and against. Disadvantages are the time-taking procedures with harmony seeking parties in the context of the decision making process with the risk of accepting less than ideal or even enforced solutions.

The polder-ethics is at odd with the fight culture as we recognize in the States. In the USA the so often heard call 'I'm gonna sue you' is a consequence of the emphasis on

[4] Wennekes W., *De aartsvaders; grondleggers van het nederlandse bedrijfsleven*; Atlas Amsterdam/Antwerpen 1993.
[5] Albeda W., N.A. Hofstra et al.,*Toekomst van de overlegeconomie*; Van Gorcum Assen/Maastricht 1993.

'blaming and claiming'. Thus we can compare the two different types of ethics as follows. (*Figure 1*)

Figure 1 *Dutch Polder Ethics versus Anglo-Saxon Ethics*

Dutch polder-ethics	Anglo-Saxon ethics
harmony	conflict
responsibility	accountability
respect	blame
deliberation	fight
prudence	proud
intentional	teleological

Although American mainstream business ethics is dominating the Dutch business ethics field, we see several opposite differences. In education systems it is rather difficult to find typical Dutch cases and for Dutch students it is rather difficult to imagine the dynamics of American society. The challenge of users of the polder-ethics model is to analyze in a systematic way Dutch business morality and it's underlying assumptions. Till today there's no streamlining of thought. Business ethics is an umbrella under which several theorists and practitioners try to improve a common consciousness of individuals: students, managers, entrepreneurs, industry, society.

Issues discussed in The Netherlands are as follows:

definitions of business ethics
research methods
moral guidelines
change ethics
corporate responsibilities
personnel management
labor relations
humanity and quality of labor
market transactions etc.[6]

---

[6] ibid A.F.Brand/E.Kimman et al 1993.

In contradiction to the Anglo-Saxon business ethics the Dutch field in business ethics is still in its infancy. No clear framework of schools can be given to contour the landscape of polder-ethics. However the first steps has been set in the low lands.

EDUCATION IN BUSINESS ETHICS

At the *Erasmus University Rotterdam Faculty of Economic Sciences* the teaching of business ethics does not have a long tradition. Rather, it does not have a tradition at all. However some lecturers do their utmost to introduce some aspects of the subject within their main courses (for example, within *Marketing, Finance* and *Business and Society*).

Although experts in the field associated with the Faculty of Philosophy in Rotterdam offer their knowledge to neighbor-economists, most of the economists refuse to acknowledge the field of business ethics to be a serious discipline. The 'Homo Oeconomicus' model still offers too much perspectives. Business ethics is not considered to be a discipline that needs a systematic and coherent treatment within organizations and within the study of economy-students. It still is the hobby of some 'Homo Ludens'. Nevertheless we can mention some more structural progress nowadays.

Firstly, within Business Economics since about five years a course is given, called *Management and Morality*. In the beginning the influence of *Etzioni* with his 'moral dimension'[7] formed the base of the course for socio-economic and business-economic students in general. Later on a more practical oriented course was given to broaden the population of students interested.

Secondly, the course *Social Business Policy*, which was focused on the internal organization, mainly human resources, evolved into the course *Business and Society*, focused on the external organization and stakeholder analyses, business ethics and sustainable development. This course has already given since 1986 and is obligated for doctorate students in Business Policy & Business Administration.

Thirdly, within the functional disciplines several courses deal with some or more ethical issues. For example *Finance and Ethics* is a course in which students discuss their reports on corporate finance, financial institutions and its ethical dimension. Besides that data-sets are provided on different subjects. For example the relationship between interest rates, income and the discussion on the social discount rate. Insider trading can be studied quantitatively and a data-set on social investments is available. In Accounting some lecturers are preparing a more ethics oriented course. Within the Marketing Department even a whole introduction for students is dedicated to *Marketing Ethics*.

---

[7] See A. Etzioni: *The Moral Dimension. Toward a New economics*. 1988. The Free Press.

It seems to be that the roar nineties will end up with a more reflective attitude for students in their study towards the next millennium. Seen from the policy of the faculty however there are hardly any stimuli for the pioneers in the business ethics field at the Erasmus University.

JOINT CONSORTIUM FOR TRANSATLANTIC CO-OPERATION

Also of particular interest is the initiative of a co-operation between European and US universities to exchange students and faculty in order to promote a development towards *sustainable growth* in business.

Business ethics will be the subject of the educational program based on the idea that recent business policy necessarily includes an understanding of the company as both an economic and a societal institution. The program has to be developed in 1998. Of special interest within the education programs will be the different perspectives the transatlantic partners will deal with. For example, the 'French view' is more philosophical and meta-ethical, compared to the more practical 'Anglo-Saxon view'.

An inventarisation and study of diverse moral systems, within different cultures as well as the development of ethical corporate responsibilities, represent the framework of the co-operation. An important novelty is the students opportunity to get acquainted with different attitudes of organizations, operating in different cultures and systems. From the Netherlands we will introduce the polder-ethics model.

The development of an analytical and diagnostic tool by Hofstra in 1994 helped students to get more grip on corporate responsibilities and corporate behavior. Since nearly four years it is used within the courses Business & Society, Management and Morality and Business Policy. Students work with it during their practical assignment. For business economists the tool has proven to work clearly. Empirical findings can be compared and discussed. (*Table 1*)

The tool is a typology that helps students to analyze and assess rather complex and abstract situations. One example is that they found a caritativ institution in culture and education that proved to be rather utilitarian. It became a scandal.

The tool helps companies to become aware of the importance of societal developments in order to ensure and create corporate viability. In the Netherlands where the government is withdrawing their social security programs it is helpful to understand the need for corporate responsiveness to societal problems.

The consciousness that profit as well as non-profit organizations play an important role in shaping contemporary societies and its rapid changes is growing. For example, the coming epoch will be the age of sustainability. Ethical guidelines are therefore indispensable.

Table 1 *An Analytic Tool for Diagnosing Corporate Responsibility and Behavior*

TYPE OF COMPANY	A-MORAL	UTILITA-RIAN	INTEN-TIONAL	VALID	INTER-ACTION
GUIDING PRIN-CIPLES	market / invisible hand	utility-principle	basic principle-ethics (justice)	virtue-ethics quality-principles	corporate responsi-bility
OBJEC-TIVES, ENDS	profit maximizing	efficiency as guideline for acting result-oriented	rights and duties, intentions behind acting	reaching the moral desired qualities	integration of economic and societal results
MEANS	competition highest profit, lowest costs	optimal allocation of capital and labour	system of rules and procedures, contracts	transparen-cy, informa-tion, internal control	reciprocal to the envi-ronment, expliciting responsi-bilities
ACTORS	Homo Oeconomi-cus, a-moral acting	common good is realised by selfish acts	actions based on general principles	the actor's character is important	character and behaviour of the actor is important
MOTIVES	maximum pleasure	optimal welfare	conscious-ness, justice and welbeing	ethical set of instru-ments	alternative ehical instruments
CORPO-RATE RESPON-SIBILITY	corporate context without moral responsibi-lity	critical limit organisation when societal costs exceed benefits	collective interests prevail over individual interest	moral restrictions in functioning	moral restrictions, reasonable, no standard
CORPO-RATE BEHA-VIOUR	tool for efficient market, no moral entity	integration of external costs and benefits	justified societal division	culture and environ-ment	pro-active strategy, learning organization
THEORIES	(neo)classi-cal, Keynesian	teleological utilitarian	deontolo-gical	virtue-based	aretaic strategic choice

We believe that ethics will be a fundament and guideline in future business policies, responsibilities and accountabilities. Besides that it is helpful in supporting strategic decision making processes. This will foster new relationship between business and society.

4

BUSINESS ETHICS IN FRANCE:

"COMMENT FAIRE SANS LA

PHILOSOPHIE?"

Yvon Pesqueux
H.E.C. School of Management
Paris

The last few years we have seen a surge of interest in ethics in the business community. Most commentaries on the subject address the following questions: Is the interest real or just a passing fad? Is business bound by moral obligations or is its concern with morality a mere mask?

In *France*, the ideological dimension of this phenomenon is taken as clear. That is why we could say that the spread of an ethics-orientated language has an ideological element and is inseparable from corporate action (real or idealized). Accordingly, this paper will show the *ideological dimension* of the language associated with ethics but also the *French specificity*. I will provide a discussion of business ethics as an applied ethics related to philosophy because of the strong tradition in philosophical research in France.

I shall first sketch the background and the evolution of the surge of interest in ethics. Next I shall examine one of the main features of the debate about ethics in France: the tendency among authors to differentiate between deontology, ethics and morality.

Lastly I shall focus on the distinctive characteristics of the French approach, namely the recourse to philosophical sources.

THE SURGE OF INTEREST IN BUSINESS ETHICS IN FRANCE

The business ethics movement in France was founded by a group of eminent persons and business leaders from various think tanks (C.F.P.C. - *Centre Français du Patronat Chrétien*, E.T.H.I.C. - another employers body, A.C.A.D.I. - *Association des Cadres de Direction*, etc.).

The movement provided a moral justification for conservative values. One of its leading figures, *O. Gélinier,* Honorary Chairman of C.E.G.O.S., played a key role in bridging the "management gap" in the post-war period by adopting American management techniques such as direct costing and management by objectives. In his book on business ethics he argued that ethics made no sense without accountability.[1]

The business ethics movement was dogged by bickering among specialists in the field which prevented the emergence of a consensus between academics and professionals as well as a separate subject in graduate management courses. And it was marked by the French intellectual tradition linking the study of business ethics with philosophy.

THE CONTRIBUTION OF FRENCH WRITERS TO BUSINESS ETHICS

Table 1 contains a profile of France's leading writers on business ethics together with a list of their publications.

Faber, in his book *"Main basse sur la cité"*[2] makes the following observations about the state of business ethics in France: The type of language used, with its claim to universality, is largely responsible for blurring the distinction between ethics and morality, thus negating the very basis of ethics. This language systematically distorts facts and introduces "noise" in the interpretation of history. For instance, business patronage of the arts is grossly exaggerated whereas the vital role played by government in supporting culture is ignored.

The ambiguity of the language allows some facts to be concealed and others to be misrepresented. For example, the image of stability projected by most firms does not square with the fact that they are continually engaged in massive asset transfers.

Faber shows that business ethics is the idealized form of the language of management by objectives, corporate culture and business excellence. He also points out that the lower one goes in an organization, the more important it is for people to be seen to believe in this language, not only because it protects them psychologically (avoidance

---

[1] O. Gélinier: *L' Éthique des affaires, halte à la dérive.* 1991. Seuil.
[2] E. Faber: *Main basse sur la cité.* 1992. Collection Hachette Pluriel.

of cognitive dissonance), but more importantly, because it helps to ward off any threat to their jobs.

Table 1 *Profile of French business ethicists*

Name	Profile	Publications
Etchegoyen A.	Professor of philosophy Founder of a firm of consultants Author of various essays on responsibility in companies and the responsibility of companies	La valse des éthiques. François Bourin Paris 1991
Faber E.	Consultant in corporate strategy at a merchant bank	Main basse sur la cité. Collection Hachette Pluriel Paris 1992
Gélinier O.	Engineer and economist Honorary Chairman of C.E.G.O.S., a leading French consulting firm	L'éthique des affaires, halte à la dérive. Seuil Paris 1991
Moussé J.	Jesuit priest Teaches business ethics and works for the Centre d'Ethique Contemporaine at the Catholic University of Lille	Fondements d'une éthique professionnelle. Editions d' Organisation. Paris 1989 Ethique et entreprises. Vuibert Paris 1993

Although government's control of business policies, their ideological bankruptcy encourages the growth of corporate language and contributes to legitimizing attempts by firms to control people's behavior at two levels: production (within the company) and consumption (outside the company).

These two activities are portrayed as indispensable to society's well-being, however unethical the actual conduct of firms (e.g. managerial practice of insider dealings to the detriment of shareholders, unethical advertising methods, etc.). Seen in this light, we can understand why business ethics is in need of philosophical buttress.

Etchegoyen opposes intelligence to morality.[3] He demonstrates the legitimacy of post-war moral criticism, arguing that, till 1945, morality served a repressive function (especially as a means of sexual repression by the bourgeoisie). He considers that morality has been transformed from a code of conduct into a language supporting grand, abstract causes (e.g. human rights). Education has undergone a similar transformation. But in condemning the hypocrisy of the old morality, it has abandoned the positive features of this morality, such as courtesy and honesty.

Managers value intelligence above morality, while turning a blind eye to the moral disintegration of politics; widespread embezzlement; scandalous medical malpractice; and daily case of cheating and fraud.

It is against this background that the surge of interest in business ethics must be understood. Having been propelled into the foreground of public attention, companies are doing their level best to shed their predatory image and portray themselves as havens of civilization. Economic theory depicts firms as predatory by nature; their drive to maximize profit and minimize costs is counterbalanced only by competition, whose role in checking excesses and promoting trade benefits the community at large. Now that they are in the spotlight, firms feel that they need to forge an identity for themselves, redefine their tasks and adopt an appropriate set of values.

For *Gélinier* business ethics is based on five postulates:[4]

(1) there is no future for unethical firms or unethical capitalism;
(2) business ethics is a money-based morality;
(3) real ethical progress consists in ethical actions not words;
(4) ethics is useless without a system of punishments;
(5) transparency is the ethical weapon of our age.

A critical analysis of literature on business ethics shows that there are two themes which are central to the subject:
- the ethics of the company in relations with its environment where justice is the moral basis for economic action;
- the role of ethics within a company where personal ethics and work ethics are mostly relevant.

THE SEPARATION OF ETHICS, MORALITY AND DEONTOLOGY

Even American scholars have acknowledged that the separation of ethics, morality and deontology is peculiar to the French view of business ethics.[5]

---

[3] A.Etchegoyen: *La valse des éthiques*. 1991. Francois Bourin.
[4] O. Gélinier: *op. cit.*
[5] Th. Donaldson: *Designing corporate ethics programs*. EBEN 6th Conference. 1993. Oslo.

Deontology and its translation into professional codes of conduct has given rise to the concept of moral responsibility among various professions (especially medicine, chartered accountants, etc.). Created by Spencer during the 19th century, this concept has been adopted in France with the specific meaning quoted above.

Both ethics and morality deal with the following questions:

- How does one distinguish between good and evil?

- What are the legitimate ends of human activity?

- What values should govern a person's action?

- What is conscience and what does it signify?

- Do rules derived from moral values apply unconditionally, whatever the circumstances?

- How does one explain the transition from values to rules, from rules to duties, from rights to law (as a concept as well as an institution) and from rights to punishment?

- What is the role of experience in such a transition?

- What is the relation between rules and duties?

Ethics and morality diverge in the following respects (*Table 2*)

Table 2 *Ethics versus Morality*

Ethics	**Morality**
deals with deeds (action)	deals with words (knowledge)
what should not be said	what should not be done
epitomized by Aristotle	epitomized by Kant
conditional	unconditional
does not relate to ends	relates to ends
does not convey meaning	convey some sort of meaning
serves as the basis of rules	serves as the basis of moral reflection

In business ethics debates in France the dichotomy of ethics and morality justifies the *use* of *philosophy* both as a source (references to the writers and ideas of philosophers) and as a method of analysis. This dichotomy also serves to assess the difference between what the philosophers actually mean and the use of them in business ethics.

Now I turn to the philosophy references and show how French commentators on business ethics reflect the interest of the authors as both academics and members of the business community. It is interesting to note that while almost all French writings on business ethics contain some reference to the American discussions, they take a markedly independent line.

TRADITIONAL MORAL REFERENCES

Adam Smith, Kant, Plato, Aristotle, Bergson, Rawls and *Habermas* are the most frequently referred authors in the French business ethics literature.

Adam Smith and the English sentimentalist school

Adam Smith is cited by all the writers as the philosopher who laid the moral foundations of economic liberalism, even though his moral thought in the *Wealth of Nations*, which forms part of his wider moral theory of sentiments, is somewhat obscure.

Gélinier, the first writer to have been "bitten" by the ethics bug back in 1965, holds that liberalism has two faces.[6] One is outdated and "primitive" which he associates with the trades union movement, social security legislation and Marxist-Leninist experiments, lumps together into the same category and rejects. The other is characterized by competition in the service of a common good. Gélinier bases himself on the argument advanced by Adam Smith in 1776 that the wealthiest countries are those whose economy and trade are free from government control. The ambitions of private entrepreneurs driven by the profit motive are checked by competition, which resolves conflicts of interest and eliminates the sort of corruption associated with the authoritarian arbitration of the Prince.

Moussé also focuses on the mechanistic aspects of "market forces", but notes that they are unsuited to the development of moral ideas.[7]

Kantian idealism

Kant's usefulness lies in the fact that he makes it possible to do away with Marx. His theories help to refute the sentimentalist approach but are grossly distorted in the process.

---

[6] O. Gélinier: *op. cit.*
[7] J. Moussé: *Éthique et entreprises.* 1993. Vuibert, Paris.

Géliner sees Kant as "a universal reference".[8] Etchegoyen distinguishes morality (the categorical imperative) from ethics (the hypothetical imperative) in order to describe "the ethical spiral" and monitors ethical developments in three areas: business, communication and bio-medicine.[9]

Faber highlights the "categorical imperative", i.e. the absolute (transcendental) nature of morality, and emphasizes the unconditionality of this imperative. He also studies the ideological forces at work behind the language used by companies to discuss moral issues.[10]

Moussé agrees with Kant's belief that one needs to act according to one's own conscience. However, he avoids direct references to Kant and deplores Kant's uncritical acceptance of the universal value of his own principles and his tendency to gloss over practical problems.[11]

Orsoni deals with the problem of following ethical rules governed by an ideal. Kant's concept of virtue is based on conviction and the dictates of an absolute moral law rather than the prospects of success of an action.[12]

Kant is clearly an indispensable reference in questions about morality and in business ethics he is systematically, even piously, quoted. He is one of the last major philosophers to have elucidated the problems of transcendence and carried the logic of his theories to the extreme.

Plato

Etchegoyen alone refers to *Plato* in the section of his book dealing with communication.[13] He quotes *Socrates'* refusal, mentioned by Plato in the *Phaedo*, to set his ideas on paper because he saw a book as a monologue in which the reader could neither answer the writer nor raise any objections. Socrates held that a book is written for rhetorical reasons and is designed to persuade rather than convince. Etchegoyen cites this argument to address the problem of communication.

It should be remembered that for Plato, ethics fulfills the same purpose as philosophy does: understanding man's actions and showing how one can make sense for them. This approach provides the conceptual framework for governing human conduct and serves as the foundation for Plato's seminal work, *The Republic*, in which he sets out the conditions for the establishment of the polis, a place where people are free to express and question opinions in public and act according to the dictates of reason.

---

[8] O. Gélinier: *op.cit.*
[9] A. Etchegoyen: *op. cit.*
[10] E. Faber: *op.cit.*
[11] J. Moussé: *Fondements d'une éthique professionnelle.* 1989. Editions d'Organisation. Paris.
[12] J. Orsoni: "L'enseignant de gestion face á la morale" *Revue Française de Gestion* 1989
[13] A. Etchegoyen: *op.cit.*

In *The Republic* there is no separation between ethics, philosophy, aesthetics and politics, the aim being to establish a polis where reason mediates between the individual and the cosmos. *The Republic* posits a method of reasoning through which man understand his nature and place in the universe. It is first through exposition, then through reasoned argument and finally through political legislation that man can create the conditions for "living together", self-improvement and a harmonious and ordered existence.

Since Plato ethics has been distinguished from morality and placed in the realm of the transcendent. Knowledge of the Good is only attained by the painstaking evolution of the spirit which moves from darkness towards light. The Good is not outside Being but constitutes the very essence of Being. Man, however, cannot attain this knowledge without first gaining an understanding of himself through the exercise of the maieutic method devised by Socrates and through contemplation of the divine.

Aristotle

For Gélinier, *Aristotle* is important because he relates ethics to ends and the means for achieving them. This is a useful approach to study the goals pursued by companies.[14]

Moussé refers to Aristotle's natural law, reduced to its factual dimension, and sees Japanese management practices as the simplest expression of natural law.[15] Orsoni cites the concept of the prudent man as a potentially vital reference in business ethics.[16] Faber quotes Aristotle to demonstrate that ethics as a human experience only has meaning if placed in its historical context.[17]

The structure of Aristotle's work establishes a philosophical break between the Good (ethics), Law (politics) and Beauty (aesthetics). For Aristotle, the Good, i.e. something that is good for its own sake and is not subject to anything else, is a useless concept for understanding or governing man's conduct. This argument was to become a critique of platonic idealism.

Aristotle introduces the idea of relativity into ethics: nothing is good for everyone at the same time. Man's destiny is no longer seen metaphorically as progress towards enlightenment but as careful navigation the purpose of which is to arrive safe and sound at one's destination and attain so much good as is adequate.

Aristotle defines happiness with a measure of realism. We cannot be happy in utter poverty and to attain happiness we must possess at least three sorts of goods:

---

[14] O. Gélinier: *op.cit.*
[15] J. Moussé: *op.cit.*
[16] J. Orsoni: *op.cit.*
[17] E. Faber: *op.cit.*

- material goods (certain possessions which protects us from hunger, cold and misery);

- bodily goods (health, reasonably good looks);

- spiritual goods (creativity, virtuous behavior)

But what principles does one use to distinguish between good actions - ones which enables us to reach our destination safely - and bad? This raises the question of justice: how to make a fair evaluation of human conduct? For Aristotle, prudence (phronesis) is the best guarantee of fairness in the evaluation of our actions and of the morality which should govern them. Prudence helps us to judge our actions in the fairest possible way and so attain happiness. Given that human nature is highly contingent and that passion (the search for pleasure, anger, loss of self-control) can at any time creep in between the knowledge of ends and attainment of the Good and happiness, prudence is indispensable. It helps us to remain balanced or on a middle course, to identify this point of harmony and, thus, to attain and preserve it.

Just as for man all happiness is only relative, so all virtue is never an absolute but only a relative value, i.e. a mean between two extremes. Prudence and justice provide the basis for the development and perpetuation of virtues in mankind, for they alone enable one to differentiate between values in a complex and contingent world where everything is relative and to distinguish right from wrong in the pursuit of the ultimate end of all human and social activity: happiness.

Aristotle thus introduces the notion of relative responsibility and leaves us to ponder over the difference between justice and equity. Equity appears more desirable than justice because it takes into account relativity and contingency - two factors that law, because of its universal character, cannot integrate. In Aristotle's writings, political ethics include a deeply human existential ethics as pure law may result in judgments that are totally inequitable. In conclusion, genuine respect of others, is the recognition of others, i.e. recognition of others as expressions of oneself, is at the root not only of justice but also of equity, its superior.

Bergson

Etchegoyen notes *Bergson's* praise of disorder at a time when morality and order went hand in hand. Indeed, moral order is a factor of revolt in its imperative dimension (as an expression of the order we receive) as well as in its descriptive dimension (as a reflection of the social order to which we belong).[18]

The starting point of Bergson's philosophy is the limitation of the pleasure principle by society. The individual self preserves, even in isolation, his social self. The usefulness of moral rules is based on the fact that one submits to them. They seek the

---

[18] A. Etchegoyen: *op.cit.*

preservation and well-being of society. Obligation is beyond the scope of reason. It stems from social practices (in contradistinction to Kant's categorical imperative which is described as purely "instinctive"). For Bergson, every obligation presupposes freedom. He distinguishes closed society (our societies) from open society (an abstract version of humanity). Unlike open societies, closed ones are driven by material considerations, building obligation on social instinct, while limiting the exercise of intelligence.

Bergson takes the example of remarkable beings (Christian saints, sages of antiquity) to show that observance of the absolute rules laid down by them is based not on mechanical solidarity, as in the case of closed societies, but on imitation of the model they propose. He introduces a distinction between social morality and human morality, both of which depend on their ability to arouse "emotions" to be effective. There are two types of emotion: one derived from an idea (supra-intellectual) and the other derived from a perceived image (infra-intellectual) akin to sensibility. While Bergson holds that emotion plays a key role in the formulation of moral law, he is in no way seeking to develop a morality of sentiment. He is interested in emotion in so far as it can be crystallized into doctrine. But doctrine is no more capable of getting people to adopt or observe morality than morality, as perceived by reason, is of making doctrine acceptable to the people. In Bergson's theory, social morality imparts an imperative quality to human morality, and the latter imparts a less social, more human quality to the former. The mercantile origins of justice make it difficult to defend the concept of infallible justice, which is a pure and simple affirmation of the law. Bergson see the gradual widening of relative justice as an approximation of absolute justice. As charity humanizes justice, it assumes the form of pure justice. Moral issues must be expressed with precision and resolved with method. But while Bergson recognizes that moral conduct has a rational character, he does not believe that morality originates in reason.

Another important feature of Bergson's philosophy is his account of moral education. The task of moral education is that of promoting the exercise of reason, defining duties and relating them to a multifaceted guiding principle. Such an education presupposes that people can and want to be conditioned (inculcation of impersonal traits) or mystic (enlightenment and spiritual union). For Bergson, "conditioning" may be an essential feature of social existence, but there are alternative forms of behavior based on religion and mysticism. Morality and religion draw their sources of inspiration from intelligence and instinct respectively.

Rawls

Rawls is quoted on account of his Kantian inspiration, which serves as a prop to the sentimentalist tradition in business ethics. Gélinier cites his two principles of justice as reference:[19]

---

[19] O. Gélinier: *op.cit.*

- equality of access under the law to the widest possible system of fundamental freedoms (equal access to inequality);

- the introduction of corrective mechanisms designed to counter inequality, benefit the least advantaged members of society and defend equality of opportunity.

Moussé considers Rawl's work as turgid and impracticable as Habermas'. However, he yet acknowledges that Rawls' ideas, though difficult to apply, are relevant to moral choice.[20]

Habermas

Etchegoyen refers to *Habermas* in his discussion of communication, especially the latter's thesis calling for people's involvement in communication as participants and not merely as observers (which raises the problem of the choice of means rather than the ends).[21]

Habermas holds that communication is a condition of morality (linked to the notion of the universalization of morality). In Habermas' thought, communication is described as the ethics of discussion. The task of morality is to prevent hatred, a view which flies in the face of Nietzsche's account of morality and confutes the theories of this taboo writer.

Moussé underlines the need for business ethics to surpass the values of legitimacy and efficiency. He uses Habermas to formulate his concept of ethics, which is based on three values: truth, justice and sincerity.[22]

According to Habermas, efficiency is the outcome of goal attainment and rational organisation (Zweckrational). This first level of efficiency has an ethical significance only in relation to a second level which incorporates all aspects of personal and social existence (the level of values - Wertrational). Habermas calls for the replacement of attitudes of domination and servitude in economic and professional life with a free and liberating attitude as the basis of decision. Business ethics, like Habermas' ethics, are all about attitudes.

For Moussé, Habermas' work is a continuation of the work of Kant. He notes that Habermas' approach is an extension of Kant's thought and that Kant's concept of achievable order can be found in Habermas.[23]

Moussé disagree with Habermas' view that ethical progress depends on exchange between people. In his *"Ethique et entreprises"* he discusses the applicability of

---

[20] J. Moussé: "Les chemins de l'éthique" *Revue Française de Gestion* 1992.

[21] A.Etchegoyen: *op.cit.*

[22] J. Moussé: *Ethique et entreprises.*

[23] J. Moussé: *Fondements d'une éthique professionnelle.*

Habermas' theories to business ethics and criticizes him for being abstract and difficult to understand.[24]

For Habermas, communicative action involves treating the other person as a subject not an object. This is what distinguishes it from sheer manipulation. He challenges the utilitarian ideas dominating game theory, the sociology of organizations and classical economics. Nor does he believe that the teleological view (the pursuit of selfish interests) is the last word on the subject of social action. Instead, he posits the vital importance of mutual understanding: only a process of discussion allows actors to adopt a meaningful strategy.

Habermas' formal pragmatism aims at a formulation of the preconditions for all ideal communication: the participants in a communication situation must agree to submit to the non-coercive constraint of the best argument. The greatest virtue of this model is its usefulness as a vehicle for genuine communication, whereby people are able to make sense of each other's actions. At the heart of this reasoning lies a complex theory of argument and action, comprising varying forms of recognition and contention. Habermas goes on to posit three sets of major claims to validity (the three moral categories): the claim to true knowledge, the claim to exactness and the claim to genuine self-expression.

Communicative action forms the very basis of social integration. The interacting subject perceives itself as an embodiment of a set of cultural beliefs and representations of reality, as an ethical being (i.e. one that conforms to the norms of society) and as a being striving for self-fulfillment in conformity with an image of the self. The experiences and environment shared by a social group, its way of relating to the outside world, its taboos and judgments as well as its devices for promoting mutual recognition among its members are all based on the consensus established or presupposed by communicative action.

Communicative action is a political concept that serves to define the concept of democracy, understood neither as a system of checks and balances, nor as the protection of private freedoms nor indeed as a set of rules reflecting a compromise between conflicting interests. It is a political condition whose legitimacy is based on discussion that is free from domination. Habermas thinks of political practice as a continuous process that aims not at the attainment of some historical end but at the proposition of debate in society (the emphasis is on "how" not "what").

CONCLUSION

The aim of the foregoing summary was to reveal the sources of writers on business ethics as well as the ideological treatment (reductionism and generalization) to which these philosophers are subjected. That is why we have to point out the *ambiguity* of the *situation* in France.

---

[24] J. Moussé: *Ethique et entreprises*.

Anyone with an interest in philosophy will perhaps feel that too much fuss has been made, in business ethics, of the idealistic notion of the company as not just a creator of wealth, a guarantor of material and technical progress, and a force for man's security and well-being, but a source of unity and solidarity for its different players, a means of overcoming man's innate selfishness, a worthy subject of philosophic inquiry, in short, a generator of freedom. For a businessman, on the other hand, such an assumption might produce a completely different, if not opposite, reaction. It is easy to emphasize the problems faced by a company (which are none other than the harsh realities of life) and to criticize the shortcomings and misdeeds of the men who interact there. What is less clear is how such problems can be used by theorists to explain, question or conceptualize corporate behavior, and how the insights so gained can illuminate the concepts of the citizen company, obligation and necessity.

Some hold that the company is the scene of an "economic nightmare", the clearest and most significant embodiment today of the evil which afflicts humanity. Such a doomsday view of the economy merely serves to justify the rejection of the world of business on ethical grounds, and to deny the very concept of the citizen company. Others argue that a moral crisis has been provoked by the failure of traditional institutions embodying morality in the public mind. But fortunately, so the argument goes, there is a healthy crop of companies capable of generating new values or resuscitating former ones which have been ignored or spurned by blindly critical theorists. This criticism and apology embody two fundamentally dichotomous and opposed schools of thought.

Fortunately, there exists a third approach derived from the observation that both company and philosophy are dangerously isolated, each cloistered in its own field and each with its own language. In spite of or because of these difficulties, there is, one might say, a double need for reconciliation: philosophy can reveal the company's hidden nature, so enhancing its understanding of its own preconceptions, especially those it is somewhat unwilling to acknowledge; and the company in turn can provide philosophy with valuable food for thought, validating philosophical approaches conceived from a very different standpoint. Some authors (mostly philosophers) are now writing in such a direction without always clearly taking the firm as a research objective but entering the discussion with business leaders[25]

Finally, I would like to make some indications about the convention between *H.E.C. School of Management* and the *Collége International de Philosophie*.

Le Collége International de Philosophie was created in the beginning of the 80's by some key philosophers in France (*Chatelet, Derrida, Lyotard* and others) to push the French School of Philosophy out of the path of erudition. In which terms would philosophers cope with the City? A convention was signed between H.E.C. School of Management and le Collége International de Philosophie with seminars organized by *Maria Bonnafous Boucher* and myself.

---

[25] F. Jullien: *Fonder la morale*. 1995. Grasset. Paris, F. Jullien: *Traité de l'efficacité*. 1996. Grasset, Paris., Y. Pesqueux et al: *Mercure et Minerve*. (forthcoming)

The first one (1996) was a Conference on the *"Ethical Evidence - critical perspectives"* with academics in Philosophy, Management and practitioners in Management.

The second one (1996-1997) was oriented on *"Ethos, Ethology and Organisations"* to discuss the ethological implicit way of looking at organizations in management. The problem of behaviorism in management has been discussed. Professor Koslowski from Germany was invited during this seminar.

The third one (1997) was based on *"Liberalism, Governmentality and Self-interest"* by reference with Foucault and because organization theory also forgets the problem of gouvernmentality in firms. Professor Berns from the Netherlands joined the previous team during this seminar.

5 FROM TEACHING TO LEARNING: BUSINESS ETHICS IN BARCELONA

Josep M. Lozano
ESADE Barcelona

The following pages describe *ESADE's approach* to education in the fields of ethics and social sciences. Teaching in these fields is an inherent part of our identity and it is our aim to make ethical and social awareness an integral part of all ESADE learning.

I will begin by describing ESADE's role in *Spain* and, more particularly, the region of *Catalonia*. I will then go on to give a brief rundown of the school's history. In the third part of the paper I will explain ESADE's approach to both the content and framework of education in the fields of ethics and social sciences. Lastly, I will discuss some of the directions we are currently exploring with an eye to developing future activities in these fields.

A KEY TO UNDERSTANDING ESADE

It is obvious to say that we cannot understand the behavior of people and institutions unless understanding their history. But this self-evident truth needs to be repeated when charting the path of business ethics in companies in Catalonia and Spain.

When the first business schools (of which ESADE was one) opened in the late 1950s, the adjective *"empresarial"* (or business) was not even listed in the official dictionaries of the Spanish language. This in itself demonstrates how far-sighted the people behind these schools actually were. With the Franco dictatorship still in power, none of the new business schools belonged to the public university system. Instead, they were the result of private initiative and usually operated under the aegis of some religious order. The 1960s were boom years in Spain and business schools played a major role in modernizing the economy, teaching new approaches to business management and attempting to develop a distinctive, non-imitative, management style of management suited to our particular social reality.

Obviously, working within political dictatorship meant that the implications of founding a business school were not just economic or professional but also had strong political connotations. To give just two examples: accepting or not accepting certain technocratic approaches (which were linked to the Franco regime's model of economic modernization) or embracing and explaining the approaches of the various labor organizations (when all but the official trade union were clandestine and actively persecuted) were not simply academic or teaching options: they were also statements about the social outlook of these business schools. Understanding this will help readers understand another highly significant phenomenon: during this time the Franco regime used the Catholic religion as a tool to legitimize its positions (which does not imply that these positions were accepted by all Catholics). Even though many of the business schools were connected to the Catholic church, not all of them made the Church's social doctrine part of their teachings, partly because this would have caused many people to believe that they were in conniving with the established order. And this was not an attractive option at a time when Vatican II was causing the Church to look at its social teachings through new eyes and more and more sectors of Catholicism were taking a critical stand against the Franco regime.

The 1970s brought hard times to Spain and many other industrialized countries (economies, ideologies, values and morals were all plunged into serious crises). At the same time Spain was also involved in shifting from dictatorship to democracy, which meant that crucial social and cultural issues took a back seat to this process, either due to the political context or interests of the time or because they were simply put off until a later date.

During the 1980s (throughout most of which Spain was governed by the socialist PSOE) both Spain and Catalonia were forced to undergo a process similar to what was taking place in other European societies, but without the support of the deep-rooted ideological and social traditions that had long existed elsewhere on the continent. In many cases the advent of moral and cultural pluralism created an atmosphere in which the pragmatic conclusion about ethics was that *"anything goes"* and there were no shared civic moral criteria. Consequently, rejection of a single, imposed moral code threatened to become synonymous with an absence of all ethical references. Despite new social problems (among them an unemployment rate that is still consistently far above the EU average) and economic challenges (adapting our businesses to the demands of the Single Market and globalization) what remained firmly planted in the minds of the public was an unfortunate mixture of the "anything goes" philosophy and a fascination with large-scale financial operations that confused "making money" (the faster and easier the better) with "doing business". Moreover, there had been a major ideological change: during the 1960s and the early 1970s the company, as an institution, was often viewed from a highly critical angle and despised as an oppressor. In the 1980s, however, the firm took on a new legitimacy at the same time as the ideological crisis broke out. Business's newly legitimized position coupled with Spain's emergence from the recession to unleash what has been aptly labeled "money madness".

Attention soon focused on certain individuals who, though by no means representative of the entire political or business community, quickly became new social role models, despite suspicions that their activities bordered on the illegal. And not only bordered...during the 1990s it was revealed that they had actually broken the law. And it has also been revealed that corruption played an important role in Spanish society and the media (some of which were not above scandal mongering in the interests of audience appeal). The fact that in recent years the governor of the Bank of Spain, the director general of the Guardia Civil, the president of a large bank and the people in charge of the finances of certain political parties have had problems with Justice is simply the manifestation of a situation that affected part of Spanish society and, above all, a good part of its collective mental models.

Obviously, over the years expectations of ethics (and business ethics) have changed. A great deal has happened in since ethics was a matter of choosing an attitude towards an official discourse that attempted to use the social doctrine of the Church to justify itself. Before, this choice was a matter of submission, critical acceptance, rejection or a search for other alternatives, while today there is so much pluralism and diversity that the search is now for common, shareable ethical references and society is demanding that certain basic values be applied to professional practices. Throughout the intervening years, business schools and, specifically, business ethics have taken their own paths. It is sufficient here to say that until very recently business ethics was not part of the curriculum in the public universities (and is now taught only in a very few): the bulk of university teaching in ethics continues to be restricted to private schools.

However, in recent years lectures, conferences and debates on the subject have proliferated. Foundations and other organizations have been set up with the specific purpose of studying business ethics. *Economía, Ética y Dirección* (the Spanish branch of EBEN) has been operating for a number of years and its members include many of the people who are attempting to respond to the practical challenges of applying ethics in Spain's companies and organizations. And what is even more important is that in Spain and Catalonia there are a variety of philosophical, economic and social approaches to business ethics, which makes for a remarkably rich field of discussion and debate.

THE ESADE APPROACH

In 1954, members of the Catalan business and professional community decided to found a university-level institution in *Barcelona* which would be dedicated to research and education in the field of management, training people capable of creating and running all types of businesses and organizations in accordance with a social and *Christian vision* of the *person* as an integral whole.

1958 saw the birth of the foundation that worked together with the *Society of Jesus* to create what is now the *ESADE Business School*. Since the very outset, one of the distinctive features of an ESADE education has been the inclusion of studies aimed at fostering a critical analysis of society. The emphasis is not on applied or professional ethics, but on analyzing social reality and attempting to provide an understanding of the firm in its social context. In other words, we have always aimed to make our students sensitive to the realities of the society around them.

ESADE has done this without identifying with a particular doctrine or ideology. The school has never opted for an officially Catholic approach to axiological or moral issues, not even at a time when the political situation would have made this a wise course to take. On the contrary, ESADE has long been distinguished by its commitment to pluralism. Although Spain's past political situation sometimes made this difficult, the school has always accepted and respected a variety of opinions and beliefs, and this has no doubt contributed towards shaping its reputation as a progressive, dynamic institution.

To cite just two examples of ESADE's traditional pluralism, tolerance and social commitment: during the political transition when the current president of the Catalan government publicly announced his political project, he chose to do it at ESADE. Also, and even before the transition years, there was room at ESADE for the oppressed labor organizations and for a few faculty members who, though professed Marxists and communists, were able to freely air their ideas and opinions in our classrooms. It could be said then that ethical and social education at ESADE has historically been less a matter of normative content than a particular attitude - an attitude that is more than just a vague open-mindedness and is instead a specific commitment to the unrenounceable basic human values.

From the very beginning ESADE opted for an international focus. A founding member of the *European Foundation for Management Development* (EFMD) and the *Community of European Management Schools* (CEMS), ESADE is also a member of the *Latin American Council of Business Schools* (CLADEA), the *American Assembly of Collegiate Schools of Business* (AACSB) and numerous other academic and professional associations.

In 1992, The *Fundació* ESADE joined the *Universitat Ramon Llull*, a federation of long-established private schools of higher education that was formed in 1991, and took responsibility for the university's teaching and research programs in legal science, creating the ESADE Law School which enhances the standard curriculum with a particular emphasis on international and business law. In 1995, the ESADE Business School also joined the *Universitat Ramon Llull*, bringing the number of federated schools to 12, with a total enrollment of 14,000 students.

Currently, ESADE describes its aim as follows: ESADE is a private university institution that combines a clearly international outlook with a fundamental spirit of loyalty and service to Catalonia and Spain. Its mission is to foster a scientific and human approach to research and education in the fields of business administration, law and the social sciences in general, preparing men and women who are able to maintain a critical attitude to their professions while striving to achieve full realization of their potential as human beings and contributing to the betterment of society. This mission further includes shaping an attitude of solidarity and service in a plural and democratic context and within the framework of the school's humanistic and Christian traditions.

THE UNDERLYING PHILOSOPHY OF THE DEPARTMENT OF SOCIAL SCIENCE

The Department of Social Sciences has a conviction that a complete management education must necessarily include an understanding of the company as a social institution and the ability to understand the links between organizational and social life.

Companies and organizations play a decisive role in shaping contemporary society and its development (just as social and cultural contexts have a decisive influence on organizational and corporate dynamics). We are living in a society of organizations, and companies play a leading role in structuring this society. Moreover, this society is undergoing rapid changes which companies (and their managers) must be capable of understanding in order to ensure corporate viability and survival.

The Department of Social Sciences, then, must contribute to shaping *ethics-related thought* on the role of companies and organizations in society, their need to provide a suitable response to social reality and their obligation to help respond to the major challenges facing humanity. Our proposal therefore aims to develop our students' sensitivity to humanity and society.

Sensitivity to humanity is in line with the humanist tradition that recognizes the *dignity* of the *person* and acknowledges that this dignity may take a variety of forms. We aim to develop our students' sensitivity to human affairs by constantly encouraging them to think about how the particularities of the organizational context can be addressed; by encouraging them to think about how contemporary society fosters new relationships between the person and the company, and by encouraging them to think about the social changes that particularly affect the possibilities of making life more human. In this framework of contemporary change cultivating human qualities is realistic and effective because organizational viability is increasingly contingent on organizations acknowledging the human reality contained within their complex structures.

Sensitivity to society is in line with the tradition of justice as an expression of a social concern that recognizes that companies and organizations contribute to the development of society, shaping it and acting as elements of social change. Our aim then is to make future managers realize that this social concern can be expressed through the business world (and its very particularities). Nowadays social concern is also a demand: contemporary changes require that every institution somehow rethink its raison d'être and its contribution to society because these things can no longer be considered obvious or permanently defined.   In an interdependent world, social concern also demands an approach to social and organizational issues which is not exclusively western in outlook.

The various courses taught by the Department of Social Sciences should therefore enable our students not only to acquire knowledge but also to develop human and social skills and attitudes. We use teaching methods that provide opportunities to openly discuss the issues addressed (case studies, group discussions, lectures, role playing, etc.).   Moreover, we deliberately aim for a broader and more integrated approach (by inviting faculty from other departments to discuss current issues with our students or by collaborating with other departments on their courses).   Last but not least, we aim to constantly develop our courses, knowing that they are not based on a set body of knowledge, but deal instead with changing social and cultural trends.

COURSES TAUGHT BY ESADE DEPARTMENT OF SOCIAL SCIENCES

Over the years ESADE's Department of Social Sciences has developed its own way of teaching courses in ethics and social sciences. We work in a team whose members complement and enrich particular fields of knowledge of one another. The department currently consists of 6 full-time faculty members working in the fields of *Social* and *Political Philosophy*, *Sociology*, *Social* and *Economic History*, *Ethics* and *Business Ethics*, *Anthropology* and *Religious Studies*. In addition, the department has fifteen part-time teachers and two visiting professors.

We feel that our contribution to the different ESADE curricula should not be just a series of separate courses. Instead, we aim to give our courses a continuity and make them complement one another, although naturally we adapt both content and methodologies to the specific programs in which they are taught. Essentially we offer four courses in ESADE's regularly scheduled programs. These four courses progressively approach the issues to be addressed and are designed as two complementary units: the first consists of *Social Philosophy* and *Sociology* and the second consists of *Society, Economics and Culture: An Historical Perspective* and *The Company in Society: Ethical Responsibility.*

The *Social Philosophy* course aims to open windows to the world, examining some current social issues and exploring both their past history and the challenges they pose for the future. This course is divided into three modules.

Module 1 is entitled *The Present as a Heritage of the Past: Transformations in Industrial and Developing Societies* and includes the following themes: Introduction to History and Methodology. Fundamental Concepts of a Model for Social Analysis.

Economic Development in Western Europe. Liberal-Capitalist Societies. Liberalism vs. Socialism: Ideological Conflicts and their Contribution to History. The Capitalist Reform Process: The Frameworks of Developing Societies. World Interdependence. The North-South Contrast: Underdevelopment, Dependence and Political Projects.

Module 2 is entitled *Power and Society* and includes the following themes: Society and Political Power: The State. Legitimization, Functions and Interpretation. Civil Society and the State. Political Power and Democracy. Law and the Democratization of Political Power. Rule of Law. The Rational Construction of the State and Protection of the Individual. The Liberal State, the Social State and the Democratic State. The State and International Society: The Reality of an Interdependent World. Human Rights: Genesis and Evolution

The third and final module is entitled *Contemporary Transformations: Problems, Challenges and New Horizons* and includes the following themes: Technological and Economic Transformations (I): Legitimization and Manipulation by the Consumer Society. The Media Society. Technological and Economic Transformations (II): Developed Societies and the Challenges of Poverty and Unemployment. Socio-political Transformations: Political Parties and Governance. Social Movements: Contributions and Demands. Cultural Transformations: Ideological Crisis, Post-Modern Discourse and Neo-Conservative Thought. The Problems of Contemporary Business Culture: Surmounting Purely Instrumental Rationality. Individualism: The Legitimacy of the New Utopian Ideals. Corporate Social Responsibility.

The *Sociology* course aims to provide students with a more scientific understanding of social reality, stressing the mechanisms and social structures that underlie social processes and facts.

This course includes the following themes: Introduction and Sociological Perspective. Constructing the Social Structure. Values, Standards and Legitimization: Culture. Globalization and Inter-Culture. Social Research Methodology: A Social Research Model. Social Research Techniques. Spain's Social Reality. Social Change and Historic Action. Technological Change and Social Change. Incompatible Ideologies. The Social Base. Common Traits in a Variety of Legitimate Ideologies. Political Change and Social Change. The Spanish Transition: From Dictatorship to Democracy. Social Structure in Developed Countries. Inequality: Poverty and Social Alienation in Developed Countries. The Relation Between Business and Society.

The course *Society, Economics and Culture: An Historical Perspective* uses history to examine the contrast between human ideals and actions aimed to satisfy the material need to survive as well as the need to create social cohesion and meaning.

This course includes the following themes: A Brief Look at the History of Socio-economic Thought. Before the State (I): Primitive Man and His Society. Before the State (II): Domestication and First Steps on the Road to Statehood. The State in Ancient Times: Efficiency and War. The Origin and Spread of Democracy. Ententes Cordials and Weak Economies. Social and Psychological Matrices: Where to Place the Great Historical Change. Collective Ideals: Theory, Pre-Modern Peoples. Cultural Evolution in Ancient Times: The Rise of the Individual. From Ancient Times to the Modern Age. Technological Level: Agriculture, Trade, Industry. Structural Level: State vs. the Bourgeoisie. Cultural Level (I): Liberal Economics as an Ideology in a Scientific World. Cultural Level (II): Liberal Politics. 19th Century Culture: A Return to Collective Endeavor. Technology and Social Structure: The Return of the (Limited) State. The Inevitable Market. "Convictions": Sounding the Alert. Culture in the Year 2000 (I): The Rise and Fall of Ideologies. Culture in the Year 2000 (II): Post-modernity and Social Tasks. The Challenge of the Third World.

The course *The Company in Society: Moral Responsibility* aims to place previously discussed issues in a corporate context and demonstrate that there are specific ways to include them in business practices. At the same time, it attempts to point out business ethics' particular contribution to society.

This course includes the following themes: The Challenge of Corporate Social Legitimacy: Business Ethics as a Response to This Challenge. The Problem of Pluralism: Civic Ethics. Business Ethics: The Distinction Between Ethics of Conviction and Ethics of Responsibility. Professional Ethics in the Business World. Personal Ethics, Professional Ethics, Business Ethics. Corporate Social Responsibility. Corporate Culture and Values. The Person and the Business Firm. Ethics and Its Place in the Decision-making Process. Conclusion: An Integrated Vision of Business Ethics.

CONTRIBUTIONS TO DIFFERENT ESADE PROGRAMS

In the five-year combined *licenciatura* and MBA program the aforementioned courses are scheduled as follows: first year: *Social Philosophy*; second year: *Sociology*; fourth year: *Society, Economics and Culture: An Historical Perspective*; fifth year: *The Company in Society: Ethical Responsibility*. All of them are required courses.

The following courses are taught as part of the full-time MBA program: *Society, Economics and Culture: An Historical Perspective* and *The Company in Society: Ethical Responsibility*. Both are required courses.

Society, Economics and Culture: An Historical Perspective is taught in the part-time MBA program. In addition, there is a week-long intensive course entitled *Business and Society*. Using a methodology that aims to integrate different viewpoints, this course examines some major social problem that is directly related to business. For example: last year's course explored the unemployment problem.

ESADE also has a doctoral program in which the Department of Social Sciences offers two seminars: one entitled *Ethics and Theories of Justice* and another entitled *Social Philosophy: Personal Ethics, Civic Ethics, Professional Ethics*. These seminars aim to provide a space for reflection that complements and enriches the work involved in earning a Ph.D. in Management Sciences. The Department also offers doctoral candidates a seminar in Philosophy. Guest lecturers are invited to briefly discuss (in one or two sessions) some aspect of a wide variety of subjects related to social, ethical and cultural issues. This seminar is also a forum where ESADE faculty members customarily gather to discuss such issues.

I am unable to give a formal description of the courses the Department of Social Sciences designs for other areas of the ESADE Business School (among them the Executive Development Center and the Public Management Institute) because these courses are custom-tailored to meet the needs of their particular programs.

Lastly, it is important to stress that ESADE is increasingly being asked to do corporate consulting on ethics-related issues. Normally, these requests come from companies which are seeking to explore some specific aspect of their activity with an eye to developing an approach that addresses their axiological and ethical concerns.

For the past several years ESADE has been working on an approach and a series of methodologies designed to aid and accompany these companies as they go through the process of defining their ethical position. Such processes are often extremely complex and usually require ESADE to set up inter-disciplinary working teams that support the companies in their endeavors. This support is never standardized. Instead, we aim to adapt it to the particular needs of each company. In short, we are convinced that developing ethics in organizations is fundamentally a learning process. Our contribution, then, must be to facilitate this process, working on the basis of the reality of each company rather than attempting to impose an external set of rules or values.

CONCLUSION: FROM TEACHING TO LEARNING

For those of us working in the field of Business Ethics the standard question is: "*Can ethics be taught?*". We feel that the future's main challenge lies in changing this question for another: "*Can ethics be learned?*". Obviously, there is no contradiction between the two questions, but there is a change in perspective, a shift to an approach in which dialogue plays a leading role.

In a plural and ever-changing world where we exist in a state of anomie or with the feeling that values are being shattered, the main question is how to make talk about ethics synonymous with talk about learning processes that include a creative commitment to certain humanizing values. How can we separate talk about ethics from talk about the so-called problems of "application", where it so often seems that the aim is to move downward from discourse to reality via a process of deduction? How can we make talk about ethics synonymous with acknowledging the diversity of social practices? How can we shape an attitude that is not conformist but investigative, one that takes reality as its point of departure and moves head to seek new possibilities that will enable us to respond to humankind's increasing expectations and desires? How can we ensure that talk about ethics addresses the issue of how we can respond to the question about what we want to achieve without falling into the trap of pragmatism or technocracy on the one hand or on the other a misty-eyed idealism that sometimes seems as though the further removed it is from reality the clearer our consciences can be.

Continuing along this line, I could perhaps sum up ESADE's priorities in the field of Business Ethics in just three words: integration, evaluation and dialogue. Our current aim is to ensure that these three words define our way of understanding ethics as a learning process.

Integration: we would like our work in the field of Business Ethics to become more and more the result of an integrative effort, with different viewpoints coming together in an increasingly interdisciplinary project. We would like to integrate different dimensions - social, organizational, professional and personal without over-emphasizing, confusing or ignoring any of them. We would like to integrate a variety of approaches so that work in the field of ethics does not consist simply of choosing between rival versions of ethics but of opting for organizational practice that benefits from the contributions of many ethical traditions.

Evaluation: we would like our work in the field of Business Ethics to be clearly concerned with questions of evaluation and auditing (if we may be permitted to use this word even though it might be ambiguous in this context). We must keep ethics from being considered synonymous with eloquent phrases and lofty desires. When you come right down to it, an organization that really wants to seriously consider the ethical dimensions of its actions must be able to identify, evaluate and propose those practices and obtain results which clearly express the particular values and criteria to which this organization is committed. Business Ethics must not only enable us to provide a better answer to the question "where do we want to go?" but also to the question "how do we know that we are getting there?" The question is certainly a complex one and the response itself will probably be complex too. Nevertheless, a response will be increasingly unavoidable.

And *dialogue:* we must learn by talking to and mutually acknowledging one another. We must respond to our local and national problems while situating them in the international context. We must turn the diversity of cultures and traditions into an opportunity and we must keep this diversity from being experienced as a threat. We therefore believe that universities must be a forum, a meeting place, a space for shared discussion and thought. ESADE in particular must strive to be a place where business and ethics are publicly discussed from a true plurality of positions and a true diversity of problems explored. We must also ensure that these discussions include the full range of social and business-related themes and problems that come under the heading of ethics.

As we at ESADE see it, this accent on integration, evaluation and dialogue is the way those two basic features of our particular framework - sensitivity to humanity and sensitivity to society - can be fostered in our society and our world today. One of the things that truly encourages and stimulates us to forge ever stronger relations with our CEMS partners is, precisely, the desire to create a place where we can share our convictions and enrich our ideas in a way that is at once realistic and profound. Lastly, we believe that a concern for developing awareness of the ethical and social dimensions of business activities could be one of the defining characteristics of the CEMS.

6 INTEGRATIVE BUSINESS ETHICS – A CRITICAL APPROACH IN ST. GALLEN[1]

Peter Ulrich & Thomas Maak
University of St. Gallen

Since our life-world becomes more and more determined by economic purposes, many people are increasingly questioning the impact of economic growth, a constant economic pressure and an accelerating globalization on the social and natural environment. There is a growing awareness of the fundamental meaning of the *moral dimension* in business and society.

However, *business ethics concepts* are still discussed controversial. Some try to develop an applied ethics of business and others an economic theory of morals. Either way, there is a lack of mediation between economic rationality and ethical reasoning. Instead, we have to search for the basis for critical reflection on economic activity, i.e. the moral point of view of modern ethics, and for the locus of morality *in* economic activity as such.

These are the groundings of the integrative approach of economic and business ethics, developed at the *Institute for Business Ethics* at the *University of St. Gallen*.

---

[1] This text first appeared in the CEMS Business Review 2, No. 1, pp. 27-36. On the occasion of this book it was slightly revised and expanded.

It avoids moral shortcomings and clarifies the relation between morality and economic rationality. Against this background the paper aims at highlighting fundamental guidelines for business ethics, not yet developed in this way. They could serve as a framework not only for courses in business ethics but for the advancement and encouragement of a reflective way to deal with the normative questions of a modern market economy in general. In the following text we give an introduction in the integrative business ethics approach concluded by some remarks on business ethics activities at the University of St. Gallen as well as an outlook on future activities.

THE CALL FOR ETHICS IN BUSINESS AND SOCIETY

Today, many people are increasingly questioning the impact of economic growth on the social and natural environment in which we live. Pollution and destruction of the environment, constant economic pressure to rationalize the world of labor, as well as the hectic pace and the superficiality of a consumption-oriented lifestyle are leading many people to wonder whether economic "progress" is really improving our quality of life. Frequent examples of an unscrupulous lust for success and profit at (almost) any price and the resulting business scandals do nothing to improve public opinion on this matter. Has economic progress perhaps overwhelmed us to the point where we have lost all sense of proportion and all feeling for the pre-eminent values in (business) life?

People are finding it increasingly difficult to escape this conclusion. We are witnessing a growing need to redefine the basic values and the purpose of the way we live, and at the same time there is growing awareness of the fundamental meaning of the *moral dimension* in business and society.[2] However, the project of reconciling economic rationality with ethics to form *business ethics* is still perceived as unusual or even provocative.

Some people still ask whether "business ethics" isn't actually a contradiction in terms. Is it not "unrealistic" to expect the world of market economies – which, after all, operates according to its own "economic laws" – to comply with ethical standards as well? Many skeptics also ask whether there are after all moral claims or values which are universally valid and unequivocal. Business ethics would appear to be a difficult "undertaking" given the nature of our modern society. Let's start by taking a look at the subject as it exists in real life.

In its fundamental, practical sense, economic activity means "creating value" *(value added)*, i.e. commodities to satisfy human needs. Since any reasonably efficient economy functions on the principle of division of labor, it is of necessity governed by the rules of social interaction and distribution of profit. Socio-economic "value-creation" can thus be understood as a practice that has always been based on moral values and norms and is inescapably founded on certain ideal concepts of *the good*

---

[2] See A. Etzioni: *The Moral Dimension*. 1988. The Free Press. New York.

life and *just coexistence* between individuals. Business ethics is thus inevitably concerned with the fundamental consideration of the meaning and purpose of human existence and the moral principles on which an economy conducive to the quality of private and social life is based.

Against the background that the industrial way of life may have to be rethought *from first principles* ethics emerges as a *reflection on crisis*[3], and one which affects practically all fundamental dimensions of our world:

- the preservation of a *natural environment* that will be fit for future generations to live in,

- efforts to establish a *social environment* which offers equal opportunities and fair conditions of life to all,

- the development of a meaningful *intellectual and spiritual inner life,*

- the establishment of just and peaceful *world relations* in the face of globalizing markets.

What we are dealing with here is the epochal challenge of embedding the economic process in a meaningful ethical and political framework for the "vital" purposes of the good life in a just society. An enterprise which will even be more challenging since the process of market globalization causes aggravating circumstances.

In view of the fundamental problem of giving economic development such a practical and worthwhile dimension, the renewed receptiveness towards the ethical aspects of business comes as less of a surprise than the formerly dominant belief that economics and business management were "neutral" and "untainted" by values. A brief look at the *history of economic thought* offers some useful clues. The economic science was originally part of ethics and politics. In *Aristotle's* writings ethics, politics and economics are three parts of a whole. *Adam Smith's* classical liberal thought was influenced by the Stoics and by British deism, which placed the market firmly within an ethical, political and metaphysical concept – in contrast to the widespread but perfunctory interpretation of *Smith* as a radical *laissez-faire* economist.[4] It was not by chance that classical liberal economic theory claimed to be *Political Economy*. The idea that ethics, politics and economics formed a single unit reflected the true position of the economy within the normative confines of society.

The development of the modern economy radically changed the relationship between the economy and society. The cultural basis offered by the *Protestant work ethic*[5] was merged with the technological basis of the industrial revolution to foster a sort of

---

[3] M. Riedel: *Norm und Werturteil.* 1979. Reclam. Stuttgart p. 8.
[4] For further reflection on the "other" Adam Smith, the classic of economic ethics, see A. Mejer-Faje & P. Ulrich (eds.): *Der andere Adam Smith. Beitrage zur Neubestimmung von Ökonomie als Politischer Ökonomie.* 1991. Haupt. Berne - Stuttgart.
[5] See M. Weber: *Protestant Ethic and the Spirit of Capitalism.* 1985. Harper. San Francisco.

"unfettered" economic rationalization. The release from the normative constraints of tradition pushed society headlong into industrial modernization and gave rise to the systems character of the modern economy. The system became divorced from everyday life.[6]

Today, the *two-world concept* that developed from non-value-based "pure" economic theory on the one hand and philosophical ethics on the other hand is increasingly viewed both in theoretical and practical terms as more of a problem than an answer. As long as ethics and economics remain indifferent to and separate from each other, there can literally be no point of mediation. These two very aloof disciplines first need to be brought together systematically if economic rationality is to be set on a course that includes both ethical legitimacy *and* efficiency. The problem here is to integrate modern economics and ethics without reducing one to the other. This is by no means an ivory-towered academic problem. We should recall that there are always two sides to any *reasonable economic activity*: the question of reasonable (i.e. *legitimate*) ends and the question of finding rational (*efficient*) means to reach these reasonable ends. But what are ethically reasonable ends? To find an answer we need an enlightened understanding of the moral point of view as a category of practical reason.

WHAT IS A MORAL POINT OF VIEW?

Since business ethics addresses itself to scholars, students and practitioners who usually are not familiar with philosophical categories, we consider it to be essential to outline well-defined basics in general ethics. Only then we can avoid the shortcomings in moral reasoning which are typical for many contemporary concepts of business ethics.

Elementary concepts in philosophical ethics

The object of all ethical considerations is the phenomenon of *morals* or good behavior as it is perceived by a society. Morals are based on values and behavioral norms derived from the traditions of that culture; they determine the way life is lived, irrespective of the degree to which those who nurture a particular tradition are aware of this relationship. *Morality*, on the other hand, is the "nature" or the fundamental disposition of man as a cultural being with moral sensitivities (a conscience) and the ability to make moral judgments. Human beings fundamentally depend for their existence on moral bearings and direction. The morality of man has to be understood as an universal aspect of the human condition.[7]

The Greek term *ethos* was originally almost identical in meaning to the Latin *moral*; today it refers primarily to the subjective moral awareness that a person uses to define him- or herself and which defines the moral principles guiding the way a person lives.

---

[6] See J. Habermas: *The Theory of Communicative Action*. Vol. I. and II. 1985. Beacon Press. Boston.

[7] Cf. H. Plessner: "Conditio Humana" in G. Mann & A. Heuss (eds.): *Propylaen Weltgeschichte*. Vol. 1. Propylaen. Berlin - Frankfurt. Pp. 33-86.

The ethos of a person, a community or a profession (e.g. doctors, lawyers, entrepreneurs) incorporates all the normative convictions that create an identity, give inner meaning and direction to activities in general or a specific aspect of life (e.g. professional activity) and provide a background against which behavior is justified to others and oneself.

As distinguished from a personal ethos, modern *ethics* describes the philosophical and critical reflection on *good reasons* for the legitimization of moral claims, i.e. on reasons which appear reasonable to anyone open to rational argument. The guiding idea of ethics is thus never to impose moral teaching merely received by tradition and driven by interests or ideology but always to express reasoned criticism of morals, interests and ideologies. Modern ethics thus appears as a contribution to the critical scrutiny and continued development of moral traditions; it is a formal way of practical (normative) reasoning. This is exactly what suits to the general conditions of a modern society: Modernity means that all claims for theoretical validity (truth) and practical rightness (moral obligations) be justified, and this is why credible morals are now unthinkable without ethical reflection.

This type of reflection on good reasons, however, creates awareness of the *relativity* of culture-specific moral traditions. This is the background against which the contemporary tendency to *ethical relativism* must be understood. From the fact that competing moral traditions exist, e.g. in different cultures, the relativist draws the incorrect *skeptical* conclusion that it is quite impossible to justify any intercultural, universal moral principle. In the context of Business such practical relativism is something often found in dealings with totalitarian states from other cultures, where companies may seek to legitimize their actions with the argument that customs are simply different elsewhere. China or Nigeria are representative examples of this for the time being. Is it advisable to do business with a government that systematically and vehemently tramples on human rights? From the ethical point of view the answer is clearly no. But it seems as if global competition licenses ignorance of intercultural moral principles. If we are to avoid the perils of social and ecological dumping, we therefore need intercultural standards for the practical attainment of moral reason in international economic matters. One approach is to employ modern ethics to establish moral principles which are so fundamental in their nature that they must take precedence over every culture-specific tradition and can claim universal validity (*ethical universalism*).

Is there a universal moral point of view?

The very fact of being human provides a "platform" for an universal moral point of view: Whatever the cultural slant of moral issues and values, nobody can reasonably dispute that all individuals are human beings; it is therefore reasonable to propose the categorical preservation of human dignity and recognition of basic human rights as a minimum ethical standard which requires no further justification. It is imperative that each person be acknowledged and respected as a physically and emotionally vulnerable being, and thus that he or she should enjoy categorical protection of his or her identity and integrity. The point here is no more and no less than the fundamental *ethos of humanity.*

Humanistic ethics does not need to be derived from dogmatic or enforced "superhuman" values, since its base is a reflection on the normative logic of mutual moral claims between free people who respect each other because of their reasonable insight that in the field of human interaction they all have an equal moral right to freedom and human dignity. From this *principle of reciprocity* emerges on the modern basis of a "culture of reason" [8] the germ of an idea for a *moral point of view* that all reasonable people can recognize as valid and compelling. At the same time this is the point of view held by the *ethics of freedom,* meaning the greatest possible and equal freedom for all people. Apparently this well-considered idea of freedom includes *justice* [9].

Precisely in the competition-driven environment of a market economy, the importance of such an ethos of universal and categorical interpersonal acknowledgment and respect is abundantly clear. It also forms the basis of intra-company relationships – i.e. between employees and especially between different levels of a hierarchy – as well as of external relationships with customers, suppliers and other stakeholders.

Interpretations of the principle of reciprocity

Looking back through history, the principle of reciprocity underlying the moral point of view has found its earliest expression in the *Golden Rule*: "Do unto others as you would have done unto you." Yet, this formulation shows that the Golden Rule, found in practically all advanced cultures around the world, is not quite free from an egocentric orientation in its justification for human respect: The idea of reciprocity is expressed ultimately in terms of mutually *useful* respect and thus has a partly strategic character. The main concern here is fair conditions conducive to advantageous exchange.

It was *Kant* who first spoke of strictly *ethical* reciprocity as the moral point of view. Now, the principle of reciprocity is expressed in the Categorical Imperative formulated in terms of "ends": "Act in such a way that you always treat humanity, whether in your person or in the person of any other, never simply as a means, but always at the same time as an end."[10]

Mutual consideration is thus formulated as something that is imperative; the *categorical* precedence of the other's human dignity and autonomy over egocentric concerns is acknowledged *for its own sake.* The abstraction from the *concrete* other

---

[8] Cf. I. Kant: *Grundlegung zur Metaphysik der Sitten.* 1968. Standard edition. Vol. VII. (ed. W. Weischedel) Suhrkamp. Frankfurt. p. BA 7.

[9] See J. Rawls: *Political Liberalism.* 1993. Columbia University Press. New York.

[10] I. Kant: *op.cit.* p. BA 66 f.

to the *general* other (humanity represented by any other person) expands the principle of reciprocity into the *principle of moral universalization.*

A further developed interpretation of the principle of universalization and thus the moral point of view can be gained through *discourse ethics.*[11] Discourse ethics gives the final "language-pragmatic turn" to the reciprocity principle; the principle of universalization is no longer interpreted as a thought experiment of a single reasonable person but as the core of the moral community of adult beings who acknowledge each other as persons capable of and open to argumentation. The only legitimate (i.e. justified) behavior is then to pursue "private" interests which have passed the test of universalizability in that they give precedence to the dignity and moral rights of all those who are potentially affected. What we are talking about here is no more and no less than the "regulative idea" (Kant) of a *reasoned* (not only factual) consent between free adults on the vital, universal and normative preconditions for a well-ordered, just, and democratic society of free citizens. This legitimate societal order is in turn the prerequisite for people with a variety of different lifestyles to coexist in a socially acceptable way. Discourse ethics limits itself to the question of justifying ethically reasonable conditions and basic norms for legitimate behavior, and can thus be considered as providing a modern and practicable base of humanistic ethics. The anticipated needs of the future suggest that discourse ethics is especially well suited as a form of a global minimal ethics – a sort of "planetary macroethics"[12] that could make it possible to legitimate minimum moral standards which are interculturally valid and capable of bringing about a basic consensus in an era of growing globalization.

MODELS AND LEVELS OF MODERN BUSINESS ETHICS

As a point for critical reflection, modern business ethics must fulfill the task of generating *orienting knowledge*[13], *a guiding awareness* of reasonable purposes, principles and preconditions for business (know *what*). The *dispositive knowledge* provided by the not very "pure" sciences of business management on the other hand, is concerned solely with the question how to realize given aims efficiently or handle technical problems with the limited resources available (know *how*). As already said, rational business practice throws up technical *and* normative problems, and touches upon questions of ethical and practical reason as well as instrumental and strategic rationality. The fundamental task in business ethics is to reconcile economic rationality with ethical reason, first in principle and secondly in an institutional perspective. The crucial questions therefore are: how is the systematic role of ethical

---

[11] On discourse ethics, as founded by the German philosophers K.-O. Apel and J. Habermas, see S. Benhabib & F. Dallmayr (eds.): *The Communicative Ethics Controversy.* 1990. MIT Press. Cambridge. For a conception of "practical socio-economics" based on discourse ethics, see P. Ulrich: *Transformation der ökonomischen Vernunft. Fortschrittsperspektiven der modernen Industriegesellschaft.* 1993. 3rd edition. Haupt. Berne - Stuttgart - Vienna.
[12] K.-O. Apel: "Das Problem einer universalistischen Makroethik der Mitverantwortung" *Deutsche Zeitschrift für Philosophie* 1993. Vol. 41. pp. 201-215.
[13] J. Mittelstrass: *Wissenschaft als Lebensform.* 1982. Suhrkamp. Frankfurt.

reflection defined within or in relation to economic thought as such, and where is the locus of moral claims in the market economy and society?

Basic approaches to reconciling moral reasoning with economic rationality

Against the background of the methodological need to reconcile economics and ethics, we can distinguish three elementary approaches in business ethics (Fig. 1): (1) Corrective business ethics, (2) Functional business ethics, and (3) Integrative business ethics.[14]

Corrective Business Ethics

In corrective business ethics the argument goes that economic necessity and global competition determine the fate of the market economy (and should indeed do so to maintain order). This is why the sole task of business ethics is seen in restraining the economic drive for profit in borderline cases which raise considerable moral problems. This widely held view, which seeks to "apply" the ethical perspective to the economy, restricts the role of business ethics to a corrective factor – acting outside the economic logic – which needs to be applied in homeopathic doses as a specific "antidote" against *too much* economic rationality. However, since this understanding of rationality is not questioned as such, the result is a compromise in which economic logic is only restricted *by* ethics instead of being integrated *with* ethical reason. "Ethics as a means of correcting failures of economic rationality"[15] (market failure) wrongly presupposes that there is a defined field in which purely economic market control functions "without ethics". The mistake here is failure to realize that every conceivable form of market economy is a political arrangement and thus has to be justified *in its entirety* in terms of ethics. Market solutions to problems of social interaction and integration are on no account value-free and neutral but depend on the given relations of power and resources between the parties of an exchange contract. That is why an economic agreement on the "free" market has nothing to do with an ethically rational consensus in the sense of discourse ethics.[16]

Functional Business Ethics

The functional business ethics approach, in contrast to the corrective approach, is a *purely economic theory of morals* (moral economics).[17] It is argued that morality or morally oriented behavior can be worthwhile in business too and may be a useful idea.

---

[14] See P. Ulrich: *Integrative Wirtschaftsethik. Grundlagen einer lebensdienlichen Ökonomie.* 1997. Haupt. Berne - Stuttgart - Vienna.

[15] P. Koslowski: *Prinzipien der ethischen Ökonomie.* 1988. Mohr. Tübingen. p. 31.

[16] P. Ulrich: *op. cit.*

[17] See as a representative proponent of this approach K. Homann & F. Blome-Dress: *Wirtschafts- und Unternehmensethik.* 1992. Vandenhoeck & Ruprecht. Göttingen.

Figure 1: *Three approaches to business ethics*

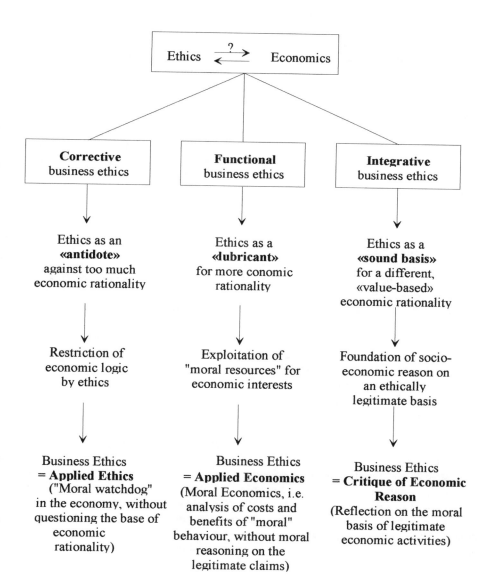

Moral economics thus analyses the *function* of morals from an economic point of view and identifies the possible benefits of certain types of behavior. The actions of the individual should be determined not by moral *intentions* (good will) but solely by their economic interest which has to be directed by the institutional framework of economic *restrictions* (incentives or "disincentives").

But this is like asking a fox to watch over the geese in ethical terms. In a strictly economic consideration morals are considered as resources or scarce goods; their absence must cause social "friction" and their production and social status benefit the economic subjects of the economy. It may of course be important and wise to show how economic subjects can be relieved of a direct moral burden through cleverly positioned economic incentives. It is, however, easy to see that systematic *reduction* of ethics to economics misses the core problem; this type of "business ethics" does not contain the vital *ethical minimum* in terms of the *imperative* moral rights of people. What if moral behavior is to no economic advantage? In that case a purely interest-based moral economy simply has no *motivation*, why the strictly self-interested player should *nonetheless* pay heed to the legitimate claims of others. Ethics *conditioned* by economics in this way cannot ultimately be considered as true ethics since the point is precisely to maintain *unconditionally* the "inviolable" basic rights and dignity of every human being.

Integrative Business Ethics

The integrative business ethics approach, as developed at the Institute for Business Ethics at the University of St. Gallen[18], starts from a critical reflection on economic reason itself, which inevitably has a normative basis. The guiding idea is to reconstruct those normative grounds in modern philosophical and ethical terms. This leads to an enlarged concept of *socio-economic rationality* that already *includes legitimacy*. In other words, the integrative approach perceives legitimacy (in the sense explained above) as a *constituting* element of overall economic reason or socio-economic rationality. Contrary to functional business ethics, the normative preconditions for legitimate business activities are considered predominant and not subordinate to economic interests, because legitimacy needs to be maintained for its own sake (and not only as a means to successful business). And in contrast to merely corrective business ethics, the integrative approach does not stop at defining moral limits to economic rationality from outside but aims at the enlightenment of the normative logic of market economies and of the prerequisites for a "life-conducive" way of doing business from within. Accordingly, integrative business ethics works as *a permanent process of comprehensive reflection on the normative preconditions of legitimate and life-conducive economic "value-creation"*. This occurs in the way of discursive moral reasoning (discourse ethics), involving all persons who are willing to reason and open to reasoned argument, above all others those affected by specific economic activities.

---

[18] See P. Ulrich: *op.cit.*

Institutional loci of integrative business ethics

In modern business ethics, the question of the institutional framework of the markets is extremely important. Business ethics can neither be based purely on an individual sense of ethical responsibility nor revolve solely around the structural question of the necessary political and societal framework; rather we have to distinguish and integrate three vertically aligned levels: (1) politico-economic ethics, (2) corporate ethics, and (3) citizen ethics. These three "loci of morality" are interdependent, but at the same time specific questions of business ethics arise on each level.

Politico-economic Ethics

Politico-economic ethics is concerned with critical reflection and implementation of general rules and a framework for the market which can be expected to culminate in overall results that are acceptable from both a human and an ecological point of view. An open and unconditioned deliberative process between politicians, business and the critical public should be encouraged to ensure that the basic market economy order is a fair and sensible one. This, however, can only be achieved if all participants have the necessary insight and good will, realizing that the process of reforming the economic and social order depends on reforms not being blocked every time the changes affect the interests of a specific group; realizing that there is basically only *one* legitimate "interest": the ethical interest in establishing general rules of legitimate competition in order to preserve the moral rights of all those involved or affected, including future generations (as the principle of justice), and to give everyone the same chances in life (as the principle of fairness).

Today, an ethically reasonable definition and implementation of a world-wide market framework presents a new and major challenge in view of the growing tendency to market globalization. This will be, however, the necessary framework within which national economic policy can be assured of creative leeway in the long term.

Corporate Ethics

Corporate ethics includes three different levels of moral reasoning in itself. First, on the *company* level the politico-economic co-responsibility of entrepreneurs and their political lobbyists has to be focused. The crucial point is that they must not adopt a "free-rider position" whenever the specific interests of their company or sector are threatened by reforms. On the contrary, willingness to share responsibility in the field of politics with regard to legitimate and life-conducive rules of competition will be a sign of integrative corporate ethics. Who, if not business players with their expertise and potential for political influence, would be able to set the necessary processes of reform in motion and even more to fulfill them? For this reason, companies and their associations bear a considerable co-responsibility for politics of economic order. They should help wherever possible to reinforce the signal and steering function of market prices, adopting general measures to pull them in a more responsible direction. The ethically enlightened use of the mechanisms by which the market is controlled is the way how companies and their associations can show their willingness to bear some of the responsibility for the general economic conditions.[19]

The next level down is *corporate dialogue* between all those affected directly by the internal and external costs and benefits of a company's activities in one word: its *stakeholders*. This is an "applied" regulative idea derived from discourse ethics. This type of *communicative business ethics* is indispensable to the extent that the entrepreneurial drive for success is increasingly being affected by the growing potential for social conflict as a result of corporate decisions and by the prospect of public resistance. The shining example of such conflict is without a doubt the "uproar" caused by Shell's plans to sink the Brent Spar oil platform. The massive protest against Shell has shown very clearly how important it is for major companies to maintain a credible relationship with all stakeholders; first and foremost for moral reasons of legitimacy, of course, but also for strategic reasons. The *Neue Zürcher Zeitung* expressed the functional side of this realization in its own distinctive style: "This means quite simply that international companies must, in their own interest, voluntarily become more environmentally friendly, transparent and ethically correct than the law requires if they are to avoid the risk of an image disaster of the type suffered by Shell." (June 25/26, 1995, p. 1) The case of Shell illustrates impressively that credibility has become one of the most important yet scarcest resources, and that pontificating "public relations" campaigns designed to gain public acceptance cannot be sufficient, what is needed is true legitimacy.[20]

The aim of communicative ethics must therefore be to establish a *potential for a dialogue of understanding* between representatives of the company and all those groups who might make legitimate moral claims on the company (customers, employees, financial backers, suppliers, the state). The guiding idea is that of the "public use of reason" (Kant) [21]: in business ethics too, the "reasoning public" is the final locus of morality[22].

Of course, corporate ethics also requires the company to act responsibly within its immediate market deals. The third part of corporate ethics therefore relates to a company's life-conducive orientation of its *business strategies* (or its "mission"). In view of the specific difficulty of reconciling ethics and economics on this level, one of the most important corporate tasks is to exploit potential syntheses between morality and (market) success. The practical starting point for such business-ethical syntheses

---

[19] In an interpretative enquiry into ethical thinking-patterns of top managers in Switzerland it was found that only a minority of about 10 % of them have reached such an understanding of business ethics, whereas many more still trust the "invisible hand" of the market, or a misconception of "private" ethics of executives. See P. Ulrich & U. Thielemann: "How Do Managers Think about Market Economies and Morality? Empirical Enquires into Business-Ethical Thinking Patterns" *Journal of Business Ethics* 1993. Vol. 12. Pp. 879-898.

[20] See P. Ulrich: "Brent Spar und der moral point of view. Reinterpretation eines unternehmensethischen Realfalls" *Die Unternehmung* 1996. Vol. 50. pp. 27-46.

[21] See J. Rawls: *op.cit.* pp. 212 f.

[22] See P. Ulrich & Ch. Sarasin (eds.): *Facing Public Interest: The Ethical Challenge to Business Policy and Corporate Communications.* 1995. Kluwer. Dordrecht, Boston, London.

is the insight that neither harmony nor conflict automatically exists between these two poles: *Not everything that is commercially advantageous is immoral, and not everything that is ethically legitimate and responsible is commercially disadvantageous!* [23] (Figure 2)

Ethical business syntheses of this kind do certainly not occur automatically, or in fact have to occur at all, so companies must pursue novel business strategies whose ethical legitimation and responsibility is founded on good (moral) reasons. This means that business decisions must not be taken solely with a view to maximum business success but also in the light of self-critical reflection on their ethical content and the practical value of alternative business strategies.

To summarize, we can identify three major *leitmotifs* of corporate ethics: the postulate of innovative syntheses within business strategies, the postulate of a dialogue-based corporate policy, and the postulate of political co-responsibility of business for the market framework.

Citizen Ethics

Citizen ethics covers three fundamental roles on the individual level of economic actors: (a) the role of a *participant in the political democracy*, (b) the role of a *member of organizations*, and (c) the role of a *reflective consumer* as well as a private *investor*. This three-way division illustrates that a person is never "only" an employee, "only" an entrepreneur or "only" a consumer or investor, but that all three roles play a special part in making up an "integral" personality within a free democratic society based on a market economy.

As a *participant in the political democracy* the citizen is aware of the importance of a free and just society and will always support the maintenance of and any necessary reforms to its rules whenever he or she perceives the need. He develops a republican ethos and self-awareness in line with Kant's idea of *civic republicanism* as the quintessence of enlightened citizenship, and acknowledges the predominance of the *res publica* – i.e. that public interest in peaceful coexistence and a just social order must override all private interests.

The subordination of private interests to the common good and, more particularly, to the basic moral rights of all people represents not an outer limit for the citizen but is understood as the underlying ethical basis of his economic freedom and legitimacy (an integrative approach!). Cohesion and justice in society are both fundamental from the individual's point of view and do not impair his autonomy in seeking a "good life"

---

[23] Cf. P. Ulrich & E. Fluri: *Management: Eine konzentrierte Einführung.* 1995. 7th edition. Haupt. Berne - Stuttgart - Vienna.

Figure 2 *The intersection model*

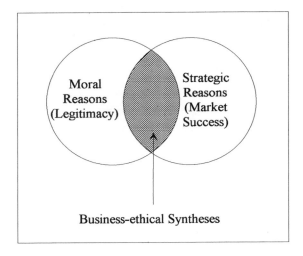

which is compatible with that of others. In other words, a balance between individualism and "communitarianism" is needed in order to ensure the *social and moral obligations between people* within communities and intermediate associations on various levels (families, neighborhoods, municipalities, associations) which represent a vital "third force" within a free and well integrated society.[24]

Citizens of a free society, as a kind of *organization* or *institution citizens* [25], should also have a right to express their opinions freely and critically within companies or other organizations for which they work, not least in view of the ethically questionable expectations which their superiors may have of them with respect to loyalty or behavior. Even though an employee should fundamentally be loyal to a company, this loyalty is overridden ethically when possible actions by the company could violate higher-ranking moral considerations or the basic rights of other people. An almost classic case in this respect would be the planned delivery of a chemical plant to a totalitarian state which could use this equipment to produce poison gas. A republican-minded management would demand *critical loyalty* from its employees under such circumstances and would institute measures (e.g. an ethics officer, ethics

[24] Cf. Th. Maak: *Kommunitarismus. Grundkonzept einer neuen Ordungsethik?* 1996. Contributions and reports from the Institute for Business Ethics. St. Gallen. No. 72.
[25] R.P. Nielsen: "Stages in Moving Toward Cooperative Problem Solving Employee Relation Projects" *Human Resources Management* 1997. Vol. 18. Pp. 2-8.

committee, or confidential ethics hot-line) to ensure that the rights of its employees were protected.[26]

And finally, in his or her role as a *reflective consumer* as well as a private *investor*, the citizen makes responsible use of the possibility of giving a "sign" to the markets, politics and fellow citizens through well-considered consumer and investor behavior. He or she will make perhaps not all but at least important and problematic purchasing decisions after considering them in ethical terms with regard to social and ecological implications. In short, he or she is aware of his or her autonomy as a critical consumer or investor and, where he or she perceives it to be necessary, will exert moral pressure – individually, as part of a civil action group or as a member of a critical shareholders' association – on producers and entrepreneurs who are not (yet) pursuing legitimate moral standards.

Now, it has been shown that there are rather various institutional places for self-critical reflection on legitimate and life-conducive economic activities which have to be differentiated and combined within a comprehensive conception of business ethics, including the levels of politico-economic ethics, corporate ethics, and citizen ethics. The aim of integrative business ethics is thus to identify moral shortcomings on all levels and to develop *orienting knowledge* towards a human, a socially responsible, and an ecologically sustainable economic life. Its "core-competence" lies in the critical reflection on the normative preconditions of ethically responsible *and* economically reasonable ways of doing business, and in generating an enlightened awareness of the guiding principles of an economy "conducive to life" (Arthur Rich); i.e. one that respects human beings as "ends" in themselves, not only as economic means (Kant).

BUSINESS ETHICS ACTIVITIES AT THE UNIVERSITY OF ST. GALLEN

We would like to conclude this text by giving some information about how business ethics has been institutionalized at our university, thus, how the Integrative Business Ethics-approach is taught. Business ethics can only be successful in the sense that future managers have to be educated and trained systematically in how to generate orienting knowledge as a framework for critical reflection of business activities. Since business ethics cannot be a management tool but has to be a way of thinking, *business ethics education* is essential for the intellectual development. The Institute for Business Ethics offers on that score several courses for undergraduate and graduate students: there are introductory courses to different topics in business ethics, both lower and upper level. The main element however is a four-semester-course for students who would like to focus on business ethics. It consists in a general and historical introduction first, then there is a systematic introduction into the main problems of modern business ethics plus the determination of the *loci of morality* within a market economy; it follows a semester on politico-economic ethics, and after all a workshop on varying topics such as the future of work or a colloquium on

---

[26] See P. Ulrich: *Führungsethik. Ein grundrechteorientierter Ansatz*. Contributions and reports from the Institute for Business Ethics. 1995. No. 68. St. Gallen.

outstanding works in the field of Ethics and Economics of authors such as *Adam Smith, Max Weber, John Rawls* and *James M. Buchanan*. Finally there is a Ph.D. course every term on such topics as "Ethics and risk in the market economy", "Environmental ethics discourses", "Economy – citizen – state", "Political versus economic liberalism" or „Ethics and consulting".

Outside the university the Institute offers corporate in-house courses and meets the real demand in talks and workshops. And, whenever there is an ethical problem which attracts the critical public's attention, like for example the recent merger of the Swiss Bank Corporation and the Union Bank of Switzerland, the institute's members are asked for comments and explanatory statements in the media. It's not exaggerated to remark that in such cases the institute is one focus of public attention in the country.

In the near future, the center of activities might shift slightly more to the corporate ethics level: it just started a project on ethical investment, and a special course offer will be developed for companies, combining a systematic introduction into business ethics and case studies. Since the installment of the chair for business ethics at the University of St. Gallen in 1987 was the first one in a German-speaking country and thus a very special event, its ten-years-anniversary has been celebrated by publishing a Festschrift on *world business ethics* [21] meeting the challenge of generating orienting knowledge facing the accelerating globalization of markets.

---

[21] Th. Maak & Y. Lunan: *Weltwirtschatsethik. Globaliserung auf dem Prütstand der Lebensdienlichkeit.* 1998. Haupt. Berne - Stuttgart - Vienna.

7 TEACHING BUSINESS ETHICS AT THE UNIVERSITY OF ECONOMICS IN PRAGUE

Lidmila Němcová
University of Economics
Prague

Business ethics as an independent discipline has been developed in the world for more than 30 years. The development of this discipline in the *Czech Republic* started after the political changes which occurred in 1989. Prior to those changes ethics appeared as a domain of philosophers only and no special care was focused on applying ethical principles in the economic life of the country. Despite specific "*socialist* or *communist ethics*" serious discrepancies existed between the state ideology and everyday life.

After 1989 some negative phenomena emerged (either "surviving" from previous times or newly arising because of new specific features of the general economic transformation process), Therefore it needed to find ways and means which would be applied to achieve economic results favorable from the ethical point of view as well.

It appeared that the presentation of ethical problems to the youngest generation of students in the countries of the previous "Eastern bloc" needed to use a very broad approach because of the total lack of information on various questions of morality and ethics which are common in countries where the traditional market system has been developed and where also traditional family education, the influence of religion, the mass media and publications on appropriate ethical problems etc. have not been suppressed.

Nowadays the approach to business ethics is really an interdisciplinary one where economists, managers, politicians, philosophers, psychologists, sociologists, historians as well as responsible dignitaries of universities are engaged.

THE ORIGINS OF BUSINESS ETHICS AT THE UNIVERSITY OF ECONOMICS, PRAGUE

The University of Economics in Prague is the leading university in the country oriented to economic problems. About 12,000 students are studying at its five faculties.

In 1991 a special research co-organized by the author at the University for the Czech government and for the ILO led to a surprising conclusion that it was the absence of ethics in entrepreneurship which had been very frequently mentioned as the main barrier to entrepreneurship. Disrespect for both the general welfare and the benefit of society as a whole is a further negative feature which can seriously impair the development of small businesses. The results have helped to make the decision to incorporate a special course on Business Ethics at the University of Economics since Spring 1992. In fact this new course prepared by the author of this article was the first one on this subject in the country. Naturally special courses on ethics continued to be given by the department of philosophy.

The new course was prepared in the light of experience and inspiration which the author gained during her previous stay in France, especially through contacts with some prominent *EBEN* specialists as Professor *Jean Moussé*.

The course presented a combination of both theoretical issues and practical applications where solution of ethical dilemmas in various situations of our economic and public life in the transformation process was considered.

It should be mentioned that the course has been introduced as an elective course with the extent of two hours/week. Originally it was proposed as a one semester seminar for 30 students. Because of the growing interest it was necessary to increase the number of seminars for 3 groups. The seminary form with the limited number for one group helps to discuss various problems and to have more time for individual presentations of the works made by the students themselves. The course has been gradually developed.

For some parts of the course also external experts are being invited. This makes it possible to present some specific ethical problems in business as well as various other dilemmas of wider importance. For example students are getting information about questions raised by an ethical approach to medicine. The course covers also an introduction to social ethics, public administration, and problems of non-profit organizations and foundations. Special attention is being paid to problems of ecological ethics and geo-ethics where the importance of environmental protection as well as concepts of sustainability and of nonrenewable resources can be explained. It is necessary to keep in mind that many of our present students will belong to the managers after the year 2000 and that they will be fully responsible for the new agenda of the 21st century.

Some videos are also used in the teaching process. The Czech TV made in 1994 a special program on Business Ethics consisting partially from interviews with the students of our University, and from the interview with me focused mostly on recent problems of how to increase the ethical climate in our society.

Sometimes I invite to my seminars interesting guests from abroad during their visits to Prague. Professor *Jean Moussé* from France or one specialist from the *Institute of Moralogy* in Japan were also speaking to the students in my courses.

The students have an active role in the seminar. Each of them has to make some special research. Various subjects for the research and evaluation can be chosen. In the first course in 1992 the following subjects were chosen:

- The personality of the entrepreneur

- Ethics in selling, advertising etc.

- Protection of consumers

- Chambers of commerce and their ethical aspects

- Codes for entrepreneurs

- Problems of economic competition

- Ethics in the decision making of municipalities

- Ethics in commercial law and ethics of legal consultants

- Ethics in medical care (handicapped people, abortion, doctors as entrepreneurs)

- Unemployment

- Entrepreneurship and the environment

- Current privatization problems in the Czech Republic (coupon method, the role of foreign capital and its ethical approach etc.)

- The doubtful future of unethical business.

Nowadays the students are visiting entrepreneurs and interview them about ethical dilemmas in their businesses.

Also some jubilees are used in my courses to present outstanding Czech personalities who helped already in ancient times to maintain the ethical atmosphere of our society and who can serve as good models.

DEVELOPING BUSINESS ETHICS IN THE CZECH REPUBLIC

Different ways and different reasons brought pedagogues from many Czech universities and high schools to the new discipline of Business Ethics. Also some contacts abroad made the domestic co-operation more effective. The *European Business Ethics Network* (EBEN) as well as the American organization Council for Ethics in Economics have been among the most important. In 1993 the Society for Ethics in Economics has been founded in Prague which started to organize or co-organize various seminars and conferences - some of them with an important impact on public opinion and behavior. The *Center for Ethics in Economics and Business* at CERGE - Institute of Economics in Prague was founded in 1994.

Many events helped to make the network more effective, especially the following ones. In December 1994 a one day conference on "Business and Ethics" took place in Prague. It was organized by the foundation PATRIAE together with the Center for Ethics and Economics in Business, Society for Ethics in Economics, A. Andersen Co., the American Chamber of Commerce in the Czech Republic and the Embassy of the United States of America in the Czech Republic. In the introductory block of lectures of the conference prominent representatives of the Czech public life (incl. several members of the Government) as well as several outstanding guests from abroad (incl. the US Ambassador and the EBEN President Professor H. van Luijk from the Netherlands) presented their proper views on business and ethics. In the afternoon two parallel sessions focused their attention to the problems: ethics in the entrepreneurial practice, and ethics and education. The conference can be considered as an achievement of a certain development period in the country. Since then the leaders of the political and economic life have been unable to stay apart from developing Business Ethics.

Another important milestone - especially for the support of teaching Business Ethics at various Universities in the Czech Republic - was a special two days conference organized by the University of Pardubice in February 1996. The presence of deans and other prominent specialists representing the majority of Czech universities with the economics orientation has proved the growing interest of the Czech academia for incorporating ethical disciplines into the curricula and education process. Problems of the optimal approach were discussed. Proceedings of this conference were published.

Without any doubt several important international conferences and seminars held in the Czech Republic (mostly in Prague) as two conferences of the Alliance of Universities for Democracy (AUDEM) in 1994 and 1996, AIESEC conferences or the 10th Annual Conference of EBEN in September 1997 presented excellent opportunities to become acquainted with the most fresh ideas in Business Ethics. Also contacts with the CEMS or co-operation with the colleagues from Slovakia are to be mentioned.

THE PRESENT SITUATION

The aforementioned development has lead to a growing interest for Business Ethics among the teachers at the University of Economics in Prague as well as among the top representatives of it. Nowadays several different courses are incorporated into the curricula of all faculties, mainly as elective courses. Their individual orientation depends on specific features and trends of individual faculties and departments. They are guaranteed mostly by the internal teaching staff of the University.

Table 1 brings a review of these courses (all of them for one semester).

Table 1 *Courses taught at the University of Economics in Prague*

course	guaranty
Business Ethics	*L.Nemcová*
Ethics and Etiquette	*I.Šronìk*
Ethics in Economics	*M.Bohatá* (external teacher)
Principles of Social Ethics and Ethics in Economics	*J.Vanìk*

Besides that Business Ethics have been included since 1997 as an integer part of the basic obligatory course "Management" for all students of the whole University. The new textbook of this discipline covers also a chapter on business ethics.

It is also important that in the faculty of Business Administration already the first diploma work on Business Ethics was presented and defended (in 1996). Also some research has been continuing including Czech case studies. The co-ordination of all courses is being arranged.

Let us mention also some publications promoting business ethics. Among the translated books that of A. Löhr and H. Steinmann: "Grundlagen der Unternehmensethik" or A. Etzioni: "The Moral Dimension. Toward A New Economics" and A.Rich: "Ethics in Economics" are to be quoted. An original Czech book by Ivan Šronik "Ethics and Etiquette" appeared. The Slovak books by A. Luknìè "The Fourth Dimension of Enterpreneurship - Ethics" and by A.Remišová "Business Ethics. An Introduction to the Problems" (both of them quoting an extreme number of foreign literature on Business Ethics) are of interest for all those who begin to study the new discipline. Several university textbooks mostly complementing new courses in the Czech universities (including the University of Economics) have been published in the course of last two years.

CONCLUSIONS

Ethics should be incorporated into every education system, primarily as an interdisciplinary subject oriented towards many applications in everyday life. The further development of ethical education should consist in developing ethical criteria into all respective disciplines which have a scientific orientation. It is inadmissible to isolate Business Ethics as a specialized course by ignoring ethical aspects and dilemmas in any specific economic discipline (accounting, foreign trade, marketing, finances, history of economics etc.). Each pedagogue has to present ethical principles in his own discipline. He should be an integer personality giving a personal example and demonstrating his purely ethical conviction.

In accordance with my own teaching practice of more than 6 years devoted to Business Ethics this is an exacting discipline, not presenting numerous facts but emphasizing and increasing both sensitivity and sensibility of students for ethical dilemmas and preparing them for ethical decision making and behavior in their future professional life. The student must arrive to the conclusion that he will be fully responsible (also from the point of view of ethics) for any decision of himself.

Let us conclude this review by two facts:

(a)   The Business Ethics in the Czech universities and academia has   reached an irreversible position; the situation in 1997 is completely different from that in 1992.

(b) The education in Business Ethics can help to ameliorate   ethical climate in business activities in the whole country.

8 ESTABLISHING BUSINESS ETHICS IN BUDAPEST

László Zsolnai
Budapest University of Economic Sciences

Business ethics was virtually *unknown* in Hungary before the political and economic changes in the late 1980s. The Communist party often used ethical arguments against the marketisation process and the market ideology. In the name of the so-called *socialist ethics* party officials made regular attacks on the entrepreneurs and entrepreneurial activities.

The *Hungarian discourse* on business ethics started to emerge in the early 1990s as basic institutions of market economy and political democracy has been established.

One line of the discourse is about how to *introduce* and *legitimize* standard *Western concepts* and *approaches* of business ethics in Hungary. There is a lot of debates about the possibility of developing and implementing *American style ethical institutions* for business such as ethical codices, ethical committees, and ethical training programs.

The other line of the discourse focuses on the *ethical reflection* on the *dysfunctional phenomena* generated by the transition process itself (extended black economy, wide-spread corruption, social deprivation of large crowds of people, e.g.).

Some participants of the discourse argue from a *Christian point of view* criticizing the headless liberalization and fast marketization of the Hungarian economy. Others represent some kind of a *socio-economics position* referring to the social and cultural embededdness of man and the economy. Finally, there people who take a consistent

82

ecological point of view in judging the state of affairs in Hungarian corporations and the entire economy.[1]

It can be stated that during the 1990s there were some considerable progress in the long process of *taking ethics seriously* in Hungarian business and economics.

BUSINESS ETHICS CENTER AT THE BUDAPEST UNIVERSITY OF ECONOMIC SCIENCES

The *Business Ethics Center* of the *Budapest University of Economic Sciences* was established by *Professors József Kindler* and *László Zsolnai* in November 1993. It has been hosted by the *Department of Business Economics*. The mission of the Center is to promote ideas and techniques of business ethics in *higher education, academic research,* and *business life.*

The *Director* of the Business Ethics Center is *Dr. László Zsolnai*. Full-time members are *Zsolt Boda, György Pataki,* and *László Radácsi*. Affiliated members of the Center are *Dr. László Fekete* and *Gabor Toronyai* from the Department of Philosophy and *Dr. Gyula Gulyás* from the Department of Public Administration. *Rita Ruschel* serves as secretary for the Center.

A number of well-known Western scholars serve as members of the International Advisory Board of the Center. They include *Professor Edwin M. Epstein* (Berkeley), *Professor Stefano Zamagni* (Bologna), *Professor Henk van Luijk* (Nijenrode University), *Professor Franz Hrubi* (Vienna), and *Professor Peter Koslowski* (Hannover).

Our background philosophy can be summarized as follows. *Ethics* is a relevant aspect at all levels of economic activities, from *individual* and *organizational* to *societal* and *global*. Complex economic problems require multidisciplinary approaches using models from *economics, management science, psychology,* and *ethics*. The *ecological,* the *communitarian,* and the *feminist* perspectives contribute significantly to our understanding of contemporary economic and social reality. Business ethics is practiced by the Center as a post-modern kind of scientific inquiry where *normative* and *descriptive* elements are not separated but inter-mingled.

---

[1] Import– ant publications include R. Andorka: "Homo Socio-Oeconomicus" *Magyar Tudomány* 1992. No.3., B. Farkas: "Changes of the Acceptance of Social Responsibility in the Hungarian Business Life" *Society and Economy* 1995. No. 5., L. Fekete: "On the Difference between Moral and Economic Discourse" *Society and Economy* 1995. No. 5., L. Kardos (ed.): *Üzleti etika.* (Business Ethics) 1994. Saldo Publisher., J. Kindler & L. Zsolnai (eds.): Etika a gazdaságban. (Ethics in the Economy) 1993. Keraban Publisher. J. Kornai: "Gazdaságpolitika és erkölcs" (Economic Policy and Ethics) *Magyar Tudomány* 1993. No. 3., F. Rabár: "Gazdasági elméletek és a gazdasági valóság" (Economic Theories and the Economic Reality) *Vigilia* 1994. No. 2., E. Richard: "An ethical island in a sea of bribery" *Budapest Business Journal* 1996. July 8-14., G. Toronyai: "Alasdair MacIntyre on the Managerial Character and Expertise" *Society and Economy* 1995. No. 5., L. Zsolnai: "Felelős gazdasági döntéshozatal és a természeti környezet" (Responsible Decision Making and the Natural Environment) *Vezetéstudomány* 1992. No. 5. And l. Zsolnai: "Profit vagy morál?" (Profit or Moral?) *Cégvezetés* 1993. November.

EDUCATION

The Business Ethics Center is devoted to develop University courses both on graduate and post-graduate levels.

László Zsolnai has developed and taught an *"Ethics in the Economy"* course for *graduate students* in business administration. The course includes the following topics: *deontology* versus *consequentialism*, basic *ethical motives* (self-interest, altruism, co-operation), the *"tit for tat"* strategy, *Homo Oeconomicus* versus *Homo Sociologicus*, *utility* and *morality* as co-determining factors of *economic behavior*, the *ultimatum bargaining game*, the *stakeholder* concept, paradigms of *corporate social responsibility*, *ethical institutions* of business, *negative freedom* versus *positive freedom*, *fairness* and *justice* in economic relations, elements of *environmental ethics*, the *feminist ethics* perspective, and the *"ethical fabric"* of the *Hungarian economy*. The course was reported in the *Wall Street Journal Europe*.[2]

László Zsolnai has also taught *business ethics courses* in the joint *MBA Program* of Budapest University of Economic Sciences and the *London Business School* as well as in the joint MBA Program of the *IMC - Graduate School of Business* Budapest and the *Case Western Reserve University* (Cleveland, Ohio). These courses are advanced and praxis-oriented versions of his "Ethics in the Economy" graduate course.

Zsolt Boda and *László Radácsi* has developed a *Corporate Ethics* course for *law and engineering post-graduate programs* of Budapest University of Economic Sciences. Their course basically concentrates on models and techniques of ethical self-regulation of companies.

László Zsolnai, György Pataki and *Zsolt Boda* taught *Ecological Economics* courses in the *Human Ecology Program* of the *Eötvös Lóránd University* in Budapest and in the *Environmental Management Program* of the *Gödöllő Agricultural University*. Main topics of these courses are as follows: *nature* versus the *economy, interactions* among *humans, organizations*, and *ecosystems, selfish organizations*, the *question* of *scale, responsible decision making*, the *GDP* and its *alternatives*, the problems of *ecological sustainability*.

The Business Ethics Center is active in organizing *summer schools* at the *Central European University*. In July 1997 we organized a two-week summer course under the title *"Economics and Environmental Ethics"*. Participants came from more than 13 countries. Lecturers included *John Gowdy* (Rensselaer University, New York, USA), *Henryk Skolimowski* (University of Lodz, Poland), *Wolfgang Sachs* (Wuppertal Institute, Germany), *Imre Lázár* (Semmelweis Medical School, Budapest), *Boldizsár Nagy* (Eötvös University Law School, Budapest), and *András Lányi* (Eötvös University, Human Ecology Program, Budapest).

---

[2] E. Beck: "Ethics 101: Start Them Young" *The Wall Street Journal Europe*'s Central European Economic Review 1995 November.

In July 1998 we organized another summer course under the title „*Ethics of Capitalism*". Invited lecturer were *Peter Koslowski* (Hannover Institute for Philosophy, Germany), *R. Edward Freeman* (Darden Business School, University of Virginia, USA), *Stefano Zamagni* (University of Bologna, Italy), *Lubomir Mlcoch* (Charles University, Prague, the Czech Republic), and *Wojciech Gasparsky* (Polish Academy of Sciences, Warsaw, Poland). The underlying philosophy of this course can be summarized as follows.

In the late 20th century the *legitimacy* of *capitalism* has been questioned on various grounds. The *general public* and more specifically the *affected parties* are more and more dissatisfied with the functioning of *purely profit-seeking* business activities. Dangerous modern technologies, globalisation, large-scale externalities, and ecological irreversibility call for new "social contract" between business and society.

The *stakeholder theory* represents a leading approach in today's business and public administration. The main message of the theory is that in corporate and public policy-making every individual, group or organisation, which can be affected by the policy, should be taken seriously. Not only the *legitimate interests* of the affected parties should be respected but also their *moral rights*. Corporate decision makers and public administrators have primary duties and obligations concerning the well-being of their stakeholders. Hence the ideal of *Kantian capitalism* emerges.

Stakeholder economics and *politics* has been entering into the arena of economic and political discourse. The theory has wide-ranging consequences since it addresses the very value basis of the market economy. To discuss the *moral foundations* of *capitalism* is especially important in *Central* and *Eastern Europe* where the legitimacy of the market economy is weak and vulnerable. *Privatisation* and *restitution schemes* have presented difficult social and ethical issues. The trade-off between *economic efficiency* and *social security* produces hard choices for politicians and business managers day by day. The success of the economic transition in the region depends not only on *material pay-offs* for the people but also on the *social* and *ethical acceptability* of the transforming process.

As a pre-program event of our "Ethics of Capitalism" summer school we organized a public debate with *George Soros* on his influential paper "*The Capitalist Threat*".[22] Discussants included *András Bródy* (Institute of Economics, Hungarian Academy of Sciences), *Olivier Giscard d'Estaing* (Business Association for World Social Summit, Paris, France), *Ferenc Rabár* (Busdapest Unviersity of Economic Sciences), and *Jörn Rüssen* (Kulturwissenschaftliches Institute, Essen, Germany). Soros' main argument was supported by the majority of participants: *laissez-faire capitalism* undermines the very values on which *open* and *democratic societies* depend.

---

[22] See George Soros: "The Capitalist Threat" *The Atlantic Monthly* 1997. February

RESEARCH ACTIVITIES

Business Ethics Center is engaged in diverse research activities. Its completed research projects include the following

Austrian-Hungarian comparative study

In 1996-1997 our Business Ethics Center conducted a joint research with the *Institute of Philosophy* of the *University of Economics Vienna* that focused on the *ethical attitudes* of *Austrian* and *Hungarian managers* and *economics students.*

One of the most interesting findings of the research is that Austrian and Hungarian managers have rather *different views* on the *role* of *ethical* and *social considerations* in business and economic life. Hungarian managers are *"hard-liners"* when *stakeholder issues* emerge within their firms but at the same time they think that the *state* should provide *social security.* Contrary to this Austrian managers are very *responsive* to the claims of their *stakeholders* but are basically *against* the *intervention* of the *state* in economic life.

Our collaborator, *Professor Franz Hrubi* presented the first results of the study in the *European Business Ethics Network Conference* in Prague, in September, 1997. Other publications are in preparation.

Social Aspects of the Competitiveness of the Hungarian Economy

In 1995-1997 the *Department* of *Business Economics* of the *Budapest University of Economic Sciences* conducted a major research on the competitiveness of the Hungarian economy. The research was sponsored by the *Center for International Private Enterprise*, Washington, DC. and directed by *Professor Attila Chikan.*

Within this larger project our Business Ethics Center conducted a study that explored the *social, ethical,* and *environmental problems* of the Hungarian economy in relation to its competitiveness. We asked about *600 companies* operating in Hungary. The sample was balanced by company size, ownership structure, industry category, and geographical location. Main results of our study can be summarized as follows.

(i) Before the system change the majority of Hungarians highly supported the economic liberalization in all aspects. Since 1989 this general attitude gradually changed. First, the opponents of liberalization gained considerably support from the population, and then they became opinion leaders. Now the majority of Hungarians urge the government's control over the market forces.

(ii) Three basic attitude clusters can be identified among Hungarians. About 15 % of the population belongs to a "liberal" cluster which represents the major supporting basis of the marketization of the economy. About 40 % of the population can be classified as anti-capitalist which represents a strong opposition to private property and privatization. The rest of the population, almost 50 % is highly ambivalent about the economic transition. It means that these people generally accept and support private property but want to constrain market competition because of high level unemployment and poverty.

(iii) The lack of economic growth, the wide-spread frustration of many social groups, and the decreasing standard of living for the middle class are all contributing factors to the weak legitimacy of the market economy in Hungary. The support and active involvement of ambivalent people is a major requirement in the development of the competitiveness of the Hungarian economy.

(iv) A low level of institutionalization of ethics characterizes companies operating in Hungary. Only 10 % of the companies have ethical codex. Other ethical institutions such as ethical committee or ethical training are almost non-existing at companies. This shows that the corporate ethics is still in its infancy in the Hungarian economy.

(v) In the present development stage of the Hungarian economy there is a strong correlation between the competitiveness of companies and their ethicality. The ethicality of the companies are highly context dependent. Those Hungarian firms display high level of ethicality that are operating in highly competitive Western markets. The ethicality of Western companies operating in Hungarian markets are unfortunately much lower.

(vi) The ethical infrastructure of the Hungarian economy should be developed as to attain the level of European Union that Western and Hungarian companies can produce the same level of ethicality that they are able to produce in the context of advanced market economies.

(vii) In the Hungarian economy about 25 % of the companies follow offensive environmental protection strategy. About 40 % of the companies represent defensive strategy and 35 % of the companies display low level of environmental protection.

(viii) Companies have a surprisingly high level of institutionalization of environmental protection in the Hungarian economy. 80 % of them have own environmental manager, 65 % of them provide some form of environmental protection, and 25 % of them are active in developing environmental friendly product or technology.

(ix) Due to the lack of environmental awareness and low willingness to pay of Hungarian people environmental concerns can become a competitive advantage by offensive firms and strong governmental incentives.

RECENT PUBLICATIONS

Laszlo Zsolnai, the Director of the Business Ethics Center published a paper under the title "*Moral Responsibility and Economic Choice*" in the *International Journal of Social Economics*.[3] He presented a normative model of responsible choice that is consistent with the main *psychological* and *sociological theories* of *human choice behavior*. Three irreducible aspects of complex decision situations are identified, namely the *deontological aspect*, the *goal-achievement aspect* and the *stakeholder aspect*. Responsible choice is defined by the *maximin rule*, that is, choosing the "*least worst*" alternative in the multidimensional decision space of *deontological, goal-achievement* and *stakeholder values*.

Laszlo Zsolnai also published a paper in the volume "*Business Ethics in East Central Europe*" edited by *Peter Koslowski*. In his contributing paper "*Business Ethics in Management Science*" he provided a picture about the *ethical problems* of the *Hungarian economy* including the *detrimental heritage* of the four decades of *communism* in East-Central Europe.[4]

Members of the Business Ethics Center, *Zsolt Boda* and *László Radácsi* edited a textbook in Hungarian on *Corporate Ethics*. The book contains classic papers of *American business ethicists* such as *Donaldson, Freeman, Hoffman* and others. The authors start with the *social responsibility* of *corporations* and then move into the *stakeholder theory*. They systematically analyze the *ethical institutions* of contemporary *American corporations*. Finally, the ethical problems of *multi-national corporations* are discussed in depth.[5]

Associate member of the Business Ethics Center, *Gyula Gulyás* edited a book under the title *Public Administration and Ethics* in Hungarian. The book contains papers by *Dennis Thompson, Richard Chapman, Colin Campbell* and other leading scholars in administration ethics. [6]

PLANS FOR THE FUTURE

A major plan of the Business Ethics Center is to develop a *Graduate Certificate Program in Economic Ethics* taught in English via the INTERNET. The program is part of the UNIWORLD - The Virtual University which is an American-Hungarian joint venture.

The program includes the following courses:

---

[3] L. Zsolnai: "Moral Responsibility and Economic Choice" *International Journal of Social Economics* 1997. No. 4.
[4] P. Koslowski (ed.): *Business Ethics in East Central Europe.* 1997. Springer Verlag, Berlin, Heidelberg, New York.
[5] Zs. Boda & L. Radacsi (eds.) *Vállalati etika.* (Corporate Ethics) 1997. Vezetőképző Intézet.
[6] Gy. Gulyás (ed.): *Közszolgálat és etika* (Public Administration and Ethics) 1997. Helikon.

Course [1]	*Ethics in the Economy*
Course [2]	*Ethical Decision Making*
Course [3]	*Stakeholder Management*
Course [4]	*Ethical and Social Accounting and Auditing*
Course [5]	*Freedom, Equality, and Justice*
Course [6]	*Global Business Ethics*
Course [7]	*Environmental Ethics and Business*

After completing the courses students are requested to produce a *short thesis* on a chosen ethical issue with reference to the practical problematic of their own organizations and/or their own countries.

The first course of the program will be introduced in 1998 as an experimental course.

As far as research is concerned the Business Ethics Center is engaged in establishing a larger project under the title "*The Ethical Fabric of a Transforming Economy: The Case of Hungary*". In this project we want to study the *emergence* and *functioning* of diverse *ethical institutions* within the companies and in their socio-political environment. Later on we would like to include other centers and colleagues to form a joint comparative research on the *ethical fabric* of *Europe*.

Notes on Contributors

HANS DE GEER

Hans De Geer was born in 1944 in Stockholm. He is a *historian*. He got his Ph.D. in history in 1978. His main fields of interest concerns contemporary history, like the history of management ideologies, the history of computerization and the history of industrial relations. He is also interested in business history. From 1968 to 1982 he worked in different positions at the Department of History at the *Stockholm University*. Between 1983 and 1994 he was researcher and research director at the private *FA institute* in Stockholm.

In 1990 he started a research program on Management Ideology and Norms, which evolved into a *business ethics research program*. In 1992 he organized an *EBEN Research Centers Meeting* in Stockholm. In 1994 he organized the *Ethics in the Public Service Conference* in Stockholm with over 200 delegates from 25 different countries all over the world.

In 1995 Hans De Geer, as an adjunct professor of business history and ethics, started the *Center for Ethics and Economics* at the *Stockholm School of Economics*, of which he since then is the director. He also teaches the course Business Values at the Stockholm School of Economics in Riga, Latvia. During 1991-1994 he was adjunct professor at the Department of Business Administration at Stockholm University.

Hans De Geer has been the editor of *Swedish Journal of History* and of *Scandinavian Journal of History*. He has published a number of books and articles in his main fields of research.

NEL HOFSTRA

Nel Hofstra was born on 12 September 1954 in Leeuwarden, the Netherlands. She has the first degree in education in *Economics* and *Marketing* and doctoral degree in *Business Sociology* both from the *Erasmus University Rotterdam*.

From 1970 to 1981 she worked in several companies and in secondary schools. Since 1986 she has been a lecturer at the *Department of Business Policy & Business Administration* of the Faculty of Economics of the Erasmus University Rotterdam. At present she teaches diverse courses such as *Business & Society, Business Ethics, Communication, International Marketing*, and *Strategic Management*.

She served as Chair of the *Society for Interdisciplinary Sustainability Research*. She is member of the *Dutch Committee for Industrial Relationships*. She is member of the editorial advisory board of the *"Filosofie in Bedrijf"* magazine. She served as Country Representative of the *Society for Advancement of Socio-Economics*.

Nel Hofstra was the author of one of the first books on the *management* of *environmental issues*. Also she published several books and articles in the field of *strategic management*. She is writing her thesis on *corporate sustainability* and *product stewardship* with her husband, *Luit Kloosterman*.

LUIT KLOOSTERMAN

Luit Kloosterman was born on 5 December 1950 in Groningen, the Netherlands. He has doctoral degree in *Business Economics* from the *State University of Groningen*. He worked in several companies and in a school in education for first degree teachers. Since 1985 he has been lecturer at the *Marketing Department* of the *Erasmus University Rotterdam*.

He is member of the editorial advisory board of *Export Management*. He has been co-author of *"Commercial Business Policy"*, a well known work in the Netherlands. In addition he published several articles in the field of *international marketing* and *management*.

He is writing his thesis on *corporate sustainability* and *product stewardship* with his wife, *Nel Hofstra*.

JOSEP M. LOZANO

Josep M. Lozano was born in Barcelona on 22 February 1954. He earned a *licenciatura* degree in *Philosophy* from the Universitat de Barcelona in 1980 and a *licenciatura* degree in *Theology* from the Facultat de Theologia de Catalunya in 1991. He was awarded a *Ph.D.* in *Philosophy* by the Universitat de Barcelona in 1996. He also has diplomas in Business Administration (ESADE, 1987) and Public Management (ESADE, 1991).

He has been a member of the faculty of Social Sciences at ESADE since 1986 teaching courses in *Social Philosophy* to students enrolled in the 5-year *Lic & MBA program*. Since 1994 he has also taught Business Ethics in ESADE programs. In 1995 he was appointed Director of the Department of Social Sciences.

He is a member of the advisory boards of a number of public and private foundations and other organizations. He serves as consultant to various companies addressing issues such as the development of corporate ethics and values. He is vice-president of *Ethica, economia y direction* (the Spanish branch of the European Business Ethics Network).

He directs the collection of management books published by ESADE in Spanish and Catalan. He is member of the International Board of *Ethical Perspectives* and of the Editorial Board of the *Barcelona Management Review*. He is also a member of the European Ethics Network group in charge of books on business ethics. He has published numerous articles and papers on business ethics, social philosophy and theology and is the author of four books, the most recent of which is *Ethica i empressa* (Ethics and Business).

THOMAS MAAK

Thomas Maak was born on 8 November, 1964 in Bielefeld, Germany. He studied business administration at the University of Bielefeld and the University of Bayreuth. He received his *Masters Degree* in *Business Administration* from the University of Bayreuth in 1992.

In 1993 he was working as a lecturer at the University of Dresden. Since October 1993 he has been a *doctoral student* at the *University of St. Gallen*. Since January 1995 he has been working as research assistant at the *Institute for Business Ethics* of the University of St. Gallen.

He has published numerous articles and edited the book "*Weltwirtschaftsethik. Globalisierung auf dem Prüfstand der Lebensdienlichkeit*" (1998, with Y. Lunau).

He works in the interdisciplinary field of *ethics, economics*, and *political philosophy*.

LIDMILLA NĚMCOVÁ

Lidmilla Nemcova graduated at the *University of Economics* in *Prague*. After a long teaching practice nowadays since 1991 she has taught *Business Ethics* at the same university. Her other course include small business management, non-profit marketing, and co-operatives in the free market economy.

In 1990/91 she studied at the *Université de Lyon* and *College Cooperatif* in France. Her study tours include Belgium, China, Denmark, England, Russia, Sweden, and the USA.

She is co-founder and member of the Executive Committee of the *Czech Society for Ethics in Economics*. She was a member of the Program Committee of the 10th Annual Conference of EBEN in Prague in 1997.

She was engaged in a PHARE program for promoting *women entrepreneurship*. She works together with her husband *Vaclav Nemec* in developing a new auxiliary discipline of earth sciences called *geo-ethics*.

Since 1990 she has been working for the *Nordic Society* in Prague. The society is a non-profit organization that promotes cultural and human relations of the Czech people with the Nordic countries.

YVON PESQUEUX

Yvon Pesqueux was born on 18 June 1951 in Bernay, France. He got his Masters Degree in Economics and his Doctoral Degree in Economics from the *University of Paris I* (Pantheon - Sorbonne).

He began his career at Forecast Department of the French Ministry of Finance. He then taught management at ENSEA (School of Engineers in Electronics). He joined *HEC School of Management* in 1988.

Since 1996 he organized seminars at the *College International de Philosophie* on the relation between philosophy and management. He created the journal "*Revue Ethiques des Affairs*" in which he has been the editor in chief.

He is an active member of the Association Francaise de Comptabilité. He is a member of the Editorial Advisory Board of the *Revue Comtabilité, Controle et Audit,* the *Revue Sciences de Gestion.* He belongs to the staff of the International Federation of Scholarly Associations of Management (IFSAM). He has been a member of each IFSAM World Congress.

Yvon Pesqueux has published articles and papers in management, accounting and control, and business ethics.

PETER PRUZAN

Peter Pruzan is Professor of Systems Science at the Department of Management, Philosophy & Politics, The Copenhagen Business School. He has degrees from *Princeton University* (B.Sc.), *Harvard University* (MBA), *Case-Western Reserve University* (Ph.D.) and the University of Copenhagen (dr. polit.).

He has been the president of a successful, innovative international business and has authored more than 100 articles and books on *operations research, planning, systems science, business ethics, value-based management* and *social/ethical accounting.*

He has recently completed leading a large four year research project on ethics, value-based management and ethical accounting and has played a leading role in the design and development of the new educational program at the *Copenhagen Business School: Philosopy & Economics.*

His teaching is at present centered around social and ethical accounting, corporate social and ethical responsibility and value-based management. His research goal is to integrate perspectives from management, philosophy and spirituality to develop operational and value-based approaches to leadership and ethics. Dr. Pruzan is active in international organizations that promote these themes.

PETER ULRICH

Peter Ulrich was born in 1948 in Bern, Switzerland. He studied economic and social sciences at the University of Fribourg. He graduated in 1976 with a *Dr.rer.pol.* from the University of Basel. After working for almost five years as management consultant in Zurich and a three-year scholarship from the Swiss National Science Foundation, he *habilitated* in 1986 with venie legendi for "*economic sciences and their philosophical foundations*" at the University of Witten-Herdecke, Germany.

From Spring 1984 to Autumn 1987 he held a full professorship for Business Administration at the University of Wuppertal, Germany. In 1987 he was appointed to the newly established *Chair* of *Business Ethics* at the *University of St. Gallen* in Switzerland, which was then the first chair of Business Ethics at a German-speaking faculty for Economics and/or Business Administration. Since 1989 he has been the *Head* of the *Institut für Wirtschaftsethik* at the same university (IWE - HSG).

From 1992 to 1996 he has been a member of the Executive Committee of the European Business Ethics Network (EBEN) and has initiated the 7th annual conference of EBEN in St. Gallen in 1994. Since 1997 he has been a member of the Executive Committee of EBEN Germany.

His numerous books include *Transformation der Ökonomischen Vernunft*. (1986, 3rd ed. 1993) and *Integrative Wirtschaftsethiek* (1997, 2nd ed. 1998). In English he edited the book *Facing Public Interest: The Ethical Challenge to Business Policy and Corporate Communications* (with Ch. Sarasin, 1995).

LÁSZLÓ ZSOLNAI

László Zsolnai was born on 5 May 1958, in Szentes, Hungary. He has *Masters Degree in Finance* and *Doctoral Degree in Sociology* from the *Budapest University of Economic Sciences* (BUES). He got his *Ph.D.* in *Economics* from the *Hungarian Academy of Sciences*.

From 1982 to 1987 he was Research Associate at the *Department of Sociology* of BUES. Since 1987 he has been working at the *Department of Business Economics* of the same University. Since 1995 he has been the Director of the *Business Ethics Center* of BUES.

He is also Visiting Lecturer in the *Human Ecology Program* of the *Eötvös Lorand University*. He was Director of the "Economics and Environmental Ethics" and the "Ethics of Capitalism" Summer Schools of the *Central European University*. Also, he serves as Adjunct Professor of Business Ethics in the joint MBA Program of the *International Management Center* in Budapest and the *Case Western Reserve University* in Cleveland, Ohio.

He has been an Active member of the *New York Academy of Sciences*. He is Editorial Advisory Board Member of the *International Journal of Social Economics* (Fresno, California). He serves as Country Representative of the *Society for Advancement of Socio-Economics* (Washington, DC). He is the initiator and coordinator of the *Interfaculty Group in Business Ethics* of the *Community of the European Management Schools* (CEMS).

László Zsolnai has more than *100 publications* on interrelated topics of *economics, ethics, human ecology* and *philosophy of science.*

References

Andorka, R.: "Homo socio-economicus" *Magyar Tudomány* 1992. No. 3.

Albeda W., N.A. Hofstra et al.: *Toekomst van de overlegeconomie*; Van Gorcum Assen/Maastricht 1993.

Apel, K.-O.: „Das Problem einer universalistischen Makroethik der Mitverantwortung" *Deutsche Zeitschrift für Philosophie*, 1993. Vol. 41, 201-215.

Bak, C.: *Etisk Regnskab* (Ethical Accounting). 1996. Handelshojskolens Forlag.

Beck, E.: "Ethics 101: Start Them Young" *The Wall Street Journal Europe's Central European Economic Review* 1995 November.

Benhabib, S. and Dallmayr, F. (eds.): *The Communicative Ethics Controversy*. 1990. Cambridge, MIT Press.

Boda, Zs. and Radácsi, L.: *Vállalati etika*. (Corporate Ethics) Budapest, Vezetõképzõ Intézet. 1997.

Bordum, A.: *Diskursetikken og Det Etiske Regnskab - Principper for Ledelse mellem Magt og Konsensus* (Discurs Ethics and Ethical Accounting - Principles for Management between Power and Consensus) 1997. Copenhagen Business School.

Brand, A.F. and Kimman E.: *Bedrijfsethiek in Nederland; Onderneming en verantwoordelijkheid*; Het Spectrum 1989.

Coughlin, R.M.: *Morality, Rationality and Efficiency. New Perspectives on Socio-Economics*. 1991. M.E. Sharpe, Inc.

De la Bruslerie H.: "Ethique, déontologie et gestion de l'entreprise" *Economica*, Paris 1992

Donaldson, Th.: *Designing corporate ethics programs*. VI° Conference E.B.E.N., Oslo 1993

Elkington, J.: *Cannibals with Forks. The Triple Bottom Line of 21st Century Business*. 1997. Oxford, Capstone.

Etchegoyen,A.: *La valse des éthiques*. François Bourin, 1991

Etzioni, A.: *The Moral Dimension. Towards a New Economics.* 1988. New York. The Free Press.

Faber, E.: *Main basse sur la cité.* Collection Hachette Pluriel, Paris 1992

Farkas, B.: "Changes of the Acceptance of Social Responsibility in the Hungarian Business Life" *Society and Economy* 1995. No. 5.

Fekete, L.: "On the Difference between Moral and Economic Discourse" *Society and Economy* 1995. No. 5.

Frederick, W. C., Post, J.E. et al.: *Business & Society: Corporate Strategy, Public Policy, Ethics.* 1995. McGraw-Hill Inc.

Friedman, M.: *Capitalism and Freedom.* 1962. University of Chicago Press.

Gélinier, O. : *L'éthique des affaires, halte à la dérive* - Seuil, 1991

Gulyás, Gy. (ed.): *Közszolgálat és etika.* (Public Administration and Ethics) 1997. Helikon.

Habermas, J.: *The Theory of Communicative Action,* Vol. I-II, 1985. Boston, Beacon Press.

Hjelmar, U. (Ed.): *Etisk Regnskab: En ny form for brugerindflydelse og kvalitetsudvikling i den offentlige sektor?* (Ethical Accounting: A New Way of Developing Consumer Empowerment and Quality in the Public Sector?) 1997. Frydenlund.

Hofstra, N.A., Timar E. et al.: *Milieubedrijfsvoering, problemen en perspectieven,* Samsom Tjeenk Willink, Alphen a.d. Rijn 1991.

Homann, K. & Blome-Drees, F.: *Wirtschafts- und Unternehmensethik.*1992. Göttingen, Bandenhoeck & Ruprecht.

Hjulmand, K.: *Det umuliges kunts: Politik og den politiske forbruger* (The Art of the Impossible: Politics and the Political Consumer). 1997. Copenhagen, Jyllands Postens Erhversbogklub.

Jensen, F.D.: *At Lede den Enkelte gennem det Foelles - bidrag til en praksisforankret styringsforstaelse.* (Leading the Individual through the Collective - Contributions to a Conception of Steering Rooted in Praxis) 1997. Aarhus Business School.

Jensen, H.S, Pruzan, P. and Thyssen, O.: *Den etiske udfording: om foelles voerdier i et pluralistic samfund* (The Ethical Challenge: on Shared values in a Pluralistic Society) 1990. Copenhagen, Handelshojskolens Forlag.

Jullien, F.: *Fonder la morale*. Grasset, Paris 1995

Jullien, F.: *Traite de l'efficacité*. Grasset, Paris, 1996

Kant, I.: *Grundlegung zur Metaphysik der Sitten*, standard edition, Vol. VII, (ed. W. Weischedel) 1968. Frankfurt, Suhrkamp.

Kant, I.: „Zum ewigen Frieden. Ein philosophischer Entwurf" in: *Schriften zur Anthropologie, Geschichtsphilosophie, Politik und Pädagogik 1*, standard edition, Vol. XI, (ed. W. Weischedel) 1968. Frankfurt, Suhrkamp, pp. 193-251.

Kardos, L. (ed.): *Üzleti etika*. (Business Ethics) Budapest, 1994. Saldo.

Kindler, J. and Zsolnai, L. (eds.): *Etika a gazdaságban*. (Ethics in the Economy) Budapest, 1993. Keraban.

Kornai, J.: "Gazdaságpolitika és etika" (Economic Policy and Ethics) *Magyar Tudomány* 1993. No. 3.

Koslowski, P.: *Prinzipien der ethischen Ökonomie*. 1988.Tübingen, Mohr.

Koslowski, P. (ed.): *Business Ethics in East Central Europe*. Springer Verlag, 1997, Berlin, Heidelberg, New York.

Kouwenhoven, A. van: *Inleiding in de economische ethiek*. Callenbach Nijkerk 1989.

Le Goff J.P. : *Le mythe de l'entreprise*. La Découverte, 1993

Maak, Th.: *Kommunitarismus. Grundkonzept einer neuen Ordnungsethik?* 1996. Contributions and reports from the Institute of Business Ethics, No. 72 (St. Gallen).

Maak, Th. & Lunan, Y.: *Weltwirtschaftsethik. Globaliserung auf dem Prüfstand der Lebensdienlichkeit*. 1998. Haupt. Berne - Stuttgart - Vienna.

Meyer-Faje, A. and Ulrich, P. (eds.): *Der andere Adam Smith. Beiträge zur Neubestimmung von Ökonomie als Politischer Ökonomie* 1991. Berne/Stuttgart, Haupt.

Mittelstrass, J.: *Wissenschaft als Lebensform*. 1982. Frankfurt, Suhrkamp.

Morsing, M.: *Den etiske praksis: En introduktion til det etiske regnskab* (The Ethical Practice: An Introduction to Ethical Accounting) 1991. Copenhagen, Handelshojskolen Forlag.

Moussé J. : *Fondements d'une éthique professionnelle*. Editions d'Organisation, Paris 1989

98

Moussé J. : "Les chemins de l'éthique" *Revue Française de Gestion*, mars - avril - mai 1992

Moussé J. : *Ethique et entreprises*. Vuibert, Paris 1993

Nielsen, R.P.: „Stages in Moving Toward Cooperative Problem Solving Employee Relation Projects" *Human Resources Management*, 1979 Vol. 18, 2-8.

Orsoni J. : "L'enseignant de gestion face à la morale" *Revue Française de Gestion*, juin juillet août 1989

Partridge, S.H.: *Cases in Business & Society*. Prentice Hall 1989.

Pesqueux Y., Saudan A., Ramanantsoa B., Tournand J.C. : *Mercure et Minerve (forthcoming)*

Petersen, C.V. and Lassen, M.S.: *Voerdibaseret Ledelse - et alternativ til styring, regulering og kontrol?* (Values-Based Management - an Alternative to Steering, Regulation and Control?) 1997. Dansk Industri.

Plessner, H.: „Conditio Humana" in: *Propyläen Weltgeschichte*, edited by Mann, G./Heuss, A., Vol. 1 1964. (Berlin/Frankfurt, Propyläen), pp. 33-86.

Poulsen, P.T. (ed.): *Ansvar og voerdier* (Responsibility and Values). 1997. Copenhagen, Centrum.

Pruzan, P. and Thyssen, O.: "Conflict and Concensus: Ethics as a Shared Value Horizon for Strategic Planning" *Human Systems Management* 1990. pp. 135-151.

Pruzan, P.: "The Ethical Accounting Statement" *World Business Academy Perspectives*.1995. Vol. 9. No. 2. pp. 35-46.

Pruzan, P.: "When Value is More than Money: on Values-Based Management" *Business Ethics* 1998 (forthcoming)

Rabár, F.: "Gazdasági elméletek és a gazdasági valóság" (Economic Theories and the Economic Reality) *Vigilia* 1994. No. 2.

Rawls, J.: *Political Liberalism*. 1993. New York, Columbia University Press.

Richard, E.: "An ethical island in a sea of bribery" *Budapest Business Journal* 1996. July 8-14.

Riedel, M.: *Norm und Werturteil*. 1979. Stuttgart, Reclam.

Reitter R. & Ramanantsoa B. : *Pouvoir et politique* .1985. McGraw Hill Paris.

Roscam Abbing, P.J.: *Ethiek en wetenschappen*, Sijthof Leiden 1971.

Sen, A.: "Does Business Ethics Make Economic Sense?" *Business Ethics Quarterly* 1993, Vol. 3, No 1.

Shand, A.H.: *Free Market Morality*; Routledge 1990.

Smith, A.: *The Theory of Moral Sentiments*, Liberty Class Oxford University Press 1974

Soros, G.: „The Capitalist Threat" *The Atlantic Monthly* 1997 February

Toronyai, G.: "Alasdair MacIntyre on the Managerial Character and Expertise" *Society and Economy* 1995. No. 5.

Thyssen, O.: *Voerdiledelse: Om organisationer og etik* (Values-based Management: On Organizations and Ethics). 1997. Copenhagen, Gyldendal.

Ulrich, P.: „Wirtschaftsethik auf der Suche nach der verlorenen ökonomischen Vernunft", in: Ulrich, P. (ed.), *Auf der Suche nach einer modernen Wirtschaftsethik* 1990.Berne/Stuttgart, Haupt.

Ulrich, P.: *Transformation der ökonomischen Vernunft. Fortschrittsperspektiven der modernen Industriegesellschaft*, 1993. (3rd edition) Berne/Stuttgart/Vienna, Haupt.

Ulrich, P.: „Integrative Wirtschafts- und Unternehmensethik - ein Rahmenkonzept", in: Bad Homburg Forum for Philosophy - *Markt und Moral* 1994. Berne/Stuttgart/Vienna, Haupt. pp. 75-107.

Ulrich, P.: *Führungsethik. Ein grundrechteorientierter Ansatz*, 1995. Contributions and reports from the Institute of Business Ethics, No. 68 (St. Gallen).

Ulrich, P.: „Towards an Ethically-based Conception of Socio-Economic Rationality. From the Social Contract Theory to Discourse Ethics as the Normative Foundation of Political Economy", *Praxiology - The International Annual of Practical Philosophy and Methodology*, 1996. Vol. 5, 21-49.

Ulrich, P.: „Brent Spar und der moral point of view. Reinterpretation eines unternehmensethischen Realfalls" *Die Unternehmung*, 1996. Vol. 50, 27-46.

Urich, P.: *Integrative Wirtschaftsethik. Grundlagen einer lebensdienlichen Ökonomie* 1997. Berne/Stuttgart/Vienna, Haupt.

Ulrich, P. and Fluri, E.: *Management: Eine konzentrierte Einführung*, 1995 (7th edition) Berne/Stuttgart/Vienna, Haupt).

Ulrich, P. and Sarasin, Ch. (eds.): *Facing Public Interest: The Ethical Challenge to Business Policy and Corporate Communications* 1995. Dordrecht/Boston/London, Kluwer.

Ulrich, P. And Thielemann, U.: „How Do Managers Think about market Economies and Morality? Empirical Enquires into Business-ethical Thinking Patterns" *Journal of Business Ethics*, 1993. Vol. 12. pp. 879-898.

Weber, M.: *Protestant Ethic and the Spirit of Capitalism.* 1985.San Francisco, Harper).

Weiss, J.W.: *Business Ethics. A Managerial Stakeholder Approach*; 1994. Wadsworth Publishing.

Wennekes, W.: *De aartsvaders; grondleggers van het nederlandse bedrijfsleven*; Atlas 1993. Amsterdam/Antwerpen.

Zadek, S., Pruzan, P. And Evans, R. (Eds.): *Building Corporate AccountAbility: Emerging Practices in Social and Ethical Accounting, Auditing and Reporting.*1997. London, Earthscan.

Zsolnai, L.: "Felelős gazdasági döntéshozatal és a természeti környezet" (Responsible Decision Making and the Natural Environment) *Vezetéstudomány* 1992. No. 5.

Zsolnai, L.: "Profit vagy morál? (Profit or Moral?) *Cégvezetés* 1993. November

Zsolnai, L.: "Environmental Ethics for Business" *Management Research News* 1996. Volume 19 No. 10,

Zsolnai, L.: "Moral Responsibility and Economic Choice" *International Journal of Social Economics* 1997. No. 4.

INDEX

—A—

Aarhus Business School, 12; 13; 96
Alliance of Universities for Democracy (AUDEM), 79
altruism, 22; 83
American Assembly of Collegiate Schools of Business (AACSB), 50
American corporations, 87
Anglo-Saxon ethics, 28
Aristotle, 37; 38; 40; 41; 61
Association des Cadres de Direction, 34
Austrian-Hungarian comparative study, 85

—B—

Barcelona, 47; 49; 90; 91
Bergson, 38; 41; 42
Berns, 46
Bernström, 22; 23
Boda, 82; 83; 87; 95
Bohatá, 79
Brand, 26; 28; 95
British Telecom, 9
Bródy, 84
Brytting, 21; 23
Buchanan, 74
Burma, 3; 5
business and society, 29; 53; 54
business economics, 29; 82; 85; 90; 93
business ethics, 1; 2; 3; 5; 7; 11; 12; 13; 14; 15; 17; 18; 19; 20; 26; 27; 28; 29; 30;
    33; 34; 35; 36; 37; 38; 39; 40; 42; 43; 44; 45; 47; 49; 54; 59; 60; 61; 62; 65; 66;
    68; 69; 70; 73; 74; 75; 76; 79; 81; 82; 83; 89; 91; 92
Business Ethics Center (Budapest), 82; 83; 85; 87; 88; 93

—C—

—D—

—E—

—H—

—I—

—J—

—K—

—L—

—M—